# Perfect Patchwork

## The Sew-Easy Way

# Margaret H. Nichols

 Sterling Publishing Co., Inc. New York

**Library of Congress Cataloging-in-Publication Data**

Nichols, Margaret H.
  Perfect patchwork : the sew-easy way / by Margaret H. Nichols.
    p.  cm.
  Includes index.
  ISBN 0-8069-0358-9
  1. Patchwork—Patterns.  2. Quilting—Patterns.  I. Title.
  TT835.N49    1993
  746.46—dc20                                          93-2321
                                                          CIP

Edited by Isabel Stein


10  9  8  7  6  5  4  3  2  1


Published by Sterling Publishing Company, Inc.
387 Park Avenue South, New York, N.Y. 10016
© 1993 by Margaret H. Nichols
Distributed in Canada by Sterling Publishing
℅ Canadian Manda Group, P.O. Box 920, Station U
Toronto, Ontario, Canada M8Z 5P9
Distributed in Great Britain and Europe by Cassell PLC
Villiers House, 41/47 Strand, London WC2N 5JE, England
Distributed in Australia by Capricorn Link Ltd.
P.O. Box 665, Lane Cove, NSW 2066
*Manufactured in the United States of America*
*All rights reserved*
Sterling ISBN 0-8069-0358-9

# Metric Equivalents

*MM—millimetres    CM—centimetres*

| Inches | MM | CM | Inches | CM | Inches | CM |
|--------|----|----|--------|----|--------|----|
| 1/8 | 3 | 0.3 | 9 | 22.9 | 30 | 76.2 |
| 1/4 | 6 | 0.6 | 10 | 25.4 | 31 | 78.7 |
| 3/8 | 10 | 1.0 | 11 | 27.9 | 32 | 81.3 |
| 1/2 | 13 | 1.3 | 12 | 30.5 | 33 | 83.8 |
| 5/8 | 16 | 1.6 | 13 | 33.0 | 34 | 86.4 |
| 3/4 | 19 | 1.9 | 14 | 35.6 | 35 | 88.9 |
| 7/8 | 22 | 2.2 | 15 | 38.1 | 36 | 91.4 |
| 1 | 25 | 2.5 | 16 | 40.6 | 37 | 94.0 |
| 1 1/4 | 32 | 3.2 | 17 | 43.2 | 38 | 96.5 |
| 1 1/2 | 38 | 3.8 | 18 | 45.7 | 39 | 99.1 |
| 1 3/4 | 44 | 4.4 | 19 | 48.3 | 40 | 101.6 |
| 2 | 51 | 5.1 | 20 | 50.8 | 41 | 104.1 |
| 2 1/2 | 64 | 6.4 | 21 | 53.3 | 42 | 106.7 |
| 3 | 76 | 7.6 | 22 | 55.9 | 43 | 109.2 |
| 3 1/2 | 89 | 8.9 | 23 | 58.4 | 44 | 111.8 |
| 4 | 102 | 10.2 | 24 | 61.0 | 45 | 114.3 |
| 4 1/2 | 114 | 11.4 | 25 | 63.5 | 46 | 116.8 |
| 5 | 127 | 12.7 | 26 | 66.0 | 47 | 119.4 |
| 6 | 152 | 15.2 | 27 | 68.6 | 48 | 121.9 |
| 7 | 178 | 17.8 | 28 | 71.1 | 49 | 124.5 |
| 8 | 203 | 20.3 | 29 | 73.7 | 50 | 127.0 |

# Contents

[Color illustrations are after page 64]

# Acknowledgments

Although countless numbers of individuals were involved in the creation of *Perfect Patchwork*, there are some special people who made significant contributions. I extend my heartfelt gratitude to each of the following: Doretha Franks, Nancy Barclay, Beth Atkinson, who put the words on paper—and without error! Carolyn Watson and Sachia Long, who meticulously added the illustrations for the block designs. Chris Barnett, who added the color to make them come alive. Jane Talbot and June Hinton Stegall, Ph.D., Mississippi University for Women, who critiqued the initial manuscript. Isabel Stein, my editor at Sterling, who worked tirelessly with me with patience and understanding to fine-tune the total. My children, Margaret, James T. Nichols, Jr., and his wife, Lisa. My grandchildren, Jay and Mary Margaret Turas, James T. Nichols III, and Megan and Lauren Nichols, who don't yet understand Grandmother's quilt.

*Perfect Patchwork* is dedicated to honor the memory of James T. Nichols, Sr., whose love for home and family served as my inspiration. These qualities motivate the doing of patchwork.

# — 1 —

# Introduction:
# Thinking About Patchwork

## Promises to Keep

If you are reading this book, I can safely assume you're interested in patchwork, and interest is the only condition necessary to learning the how-to of this traditional needle skill. The title of this book promises that patchwork is "sew easy." Patchwork is also fun to do. *I* promise that although it *is* easy, it is also beautiful! Surely these are reasons enough for your continued reading. I hope it will result in your enlistment as a forever-after doer of patchwork.

But "sew easy" is more than just the *doing* of patchwork. The entire process involves thinking and looking and learning and planning and *then* doing! Let me emphasize that your complete understanding of each step is important to the successful outcome of your patchworking efforts.

## Patchwork Per Se

First let's think about patchwork—patchwork per se—what it was, what it is, what it can be. In an effort to establish a background for positive thinking, let me share some things I have learned as a dedicated doer of this age-old needle skill. The generally accepted definition of patchwork emphasizes its tangible outcomes—the sewing together of small pieces of fabric to form a larger area of cloth, used originally as a quilt face.

While it is the tangible outcomes—the beautiful things you can see and touch—that move one into the doing of patchwork, it is only *in* the doing that we discover there are intangible outcomes as well. Though we can neither see nor touch them, we know the intangibles do exist, because they touch us and others through us. All patchworkers will attest to the fact that the intangible benefits may equal or sometimes even surpass the tangibles as providers of personal joy for doers and viewers alike. I will enumerate some of these intangibles near the close of this chapter. But there is something else I have also learned. When we understand how patchwork evolved, the need for response to the *was*, the *is*, and the *can be* becomes much more personal and therefore difficult to resist. And *that* is the primary focus of this "thinking" chapter: moving you into the doing of patchwork. When this happens, the *was*, *is*, and *can be* fall into place and patchwork continues to exist for the infinite pleasure of generations yet to come!

# A Short History of Patchwork in the United States

Let's look at the evolution of quilting in America. As a matter of record, we know that quilts were among the possessions brought to the New World by the Pilgrims; they were considered essential to their physical well-being. We know, too, that as the extremes of hard wear began to take their toll, these resourceful homemakers sought to extend the life of their quilts by patching over the wear and tear with bits of useable cloth salvaged from their equally threadbare clothing. Thus, we know that patchwork (and it was precisely that!) evolved out of necessity as the unique contribution of the early Americans to the world of quilts and quilting.

When we follow the development further, we note that the visible characteristics of patchwork were strongly affected by the conditions that existed during its creation. For this reason, patchwork changed very little in the period of chaos just preceding and following the American Revolution. Quilts were still made of *patches* of fabric—salvaged, traded, hoarded—patches unlike in size, shape, and color, even in weight! These quilts were durable but dull and uninteresting, used like blankets under other coverings. They were functional necessities but far from beautiful.

As fabric became more readily available, it was used first for needed clothing. The left-over scraps, collected and saved for patchwork, were cut into squares and pieced to avoid wasting even a thread. These early one-patch or "square" quilts are still popular; examples are Trip Around the World, Nine Patch and Checkerboard.

When the movement toward the west accelerated after the Revolution, the pioneer women carried their beloved scrap bags and quilt patterns with them. Soon the patchwork quilt of New England became the pieced quilt of the Middle West. Fabrics were cut into small geometric shapes, uniform in size, but contrasting in color. This introduction of shape and color gave rise to the creation of hundreds of interesting block designs that moved patchwork from the position of a somewhat dull necessity to that of a graphically beautiful art form. Many of these designs are still in use and are shared with you in this book.

During the time of the Civil War, mills produced inexpensive cloth in plentiful supply. The techniques of piecing designs in blocks made group construction of quilts a popular pastime. The blocks were pieced by individual homemakers; then they were sewn together and collectively quilted by the group. The completed quilt was presented to someone of importance within the community: the minister, the schoolteacher, a bride, or special friend. Such quilts were referred to as presentation quilts, album quilts, or friendship quilts. The blocks were usually signed by the women who created them and were, therefore, treasured keepsakes.

With the centennial of United States independence, the widespread availability of machine-made bed coverings resulted in the declining popularity of patchwork. By the late 1800s this lovely needle skill was practiced only in areas where life was simple, unsophisticated, and unhurried: principally, the remote communities of the Middle West and the isolated cabins of the Great Smoky and Blue Ridge mountains. Even so, patchwork survived. It will continue to do so! In an earlier United States, it was a reflection of the times, the people and the way they lived, their thoughts, their feelings, their beliefs and their hopes and dreams—a kind of history as viewed from the vantage point of the women involved in its making. For us today, it is still all of this.

Though the primary purpose of patchwork was functional, it also served as a means of self-expression and social interaction for women whose lives were filled with hard work and inconvenience, with drabness, with isolation and certainly with emotional trials. Patchwork is a folk art. It depicts the long-ago simplicity of country life for poor people, a life centered on home and family and bound together by strong spiritual values.

Patchwork represents honesty and independence, resourcefulness and industry, perseverance and patience, a joy in simple things. Today it serves a *decorative* purpose rather than a *functional* one. As such, it creates a mood or atmosphere in decorating that is "country." And country is comfort and warmth; country is togetherness and caring; it is informality, friendliness and hospitality. Country always says, "Come in, you're welcome!"

What then is patchwork? It is a treasured needle skill. The patchwork we know is indigenous to North America and, as a consequence, exists as our heritage from days long past. It will continue as such so long as viewers of the tangible end results are motivated to duplicate the skill because of the beauty of what they see: the quilts and coverlets, the mini-quilts, wall hangings, pillows, etc. When this occurs, the cycle of viewing and doing is continual and the perpetuation of traditional patchwork is thereby assured.

## Parallels in Verse

Whenever I think about patchwork, I also think about a lovely poem, *Endymion*, written by John Keats. This is what he says:

> A thing of beauty
>     Is a joy forever;
> Its loveliness increases;
>     It will never pass into nothingness.

I am convinced that John Keats was snuggled warmly under a beautiful patchwork quilt of some sort when he dreamed up these unforgettable lines. How else could he so accurately describe the reality of patchwork? Let's look at the parallel as I ask the following questions:

- Isn't a patchwork quilt beautiful, thus a thing of beauty?
- If so, can the memory of its beauty remain in the minds of the viewers to become a joy forever?
- And when we as viewers are moved to duplicate the beauty of a quilt we have seen, are we not in effect increasing its loveliness?
- Isn't the cycle of viewing and doing, which we thereby establish as an ongoing process, saying to us with unquestionable assurance that beautiful patchwork will never pass into nothingness because it will be duplicated, viewed and enjoyed over and over and over—a kind of ripple effect that is never-ending?

As we continue to think about patchwork, let me remind you of the earlier promises that patchwork is easy, that it is fun, that it is beautiful. Keeping these three things in mind, I want us now to direct our thinking to the term sew easy as it relates first to patchwork and then to *easy*, *fun*, and *beautiful*. And just in case you are thinking, "But can I make it beautiful?" let me assure you that you can indeed—exactly that! You may be a beginner with a first block (even a first patch) or an experienced patchworker with whole quilts to your credit; in either case, sew easy is for you!

## Overview of Sew-Easy Learnings

Sew easy is a how-to method of creating traditional patchwork that gives attention to the aesthetics of design and the skills of workmanship. Sew easy utilizes a number of techniques designed to save time without any loss of construction quality, provided by the gentle manipulation of fabric through hand-stitching.

- You will learn how to work without a pattern. A sketch or illustration is all you will need to duplicate any geometric or angular design.
- You will learn how to analyze a block design. This will speed up the doing.
- You will learn how to make a swatched paste-up to verify the effectiveness of your selection and the distribution of color and pattern within a block design.
- You will learn how to eliminate the margin of error in construction by stitching whole-cloth squares together *before* cutting them into smaller shapes for restitching into pieced squares.
- You will learn how to create an heirloom every time—one that will provide viewing pleasure for generations yet to come—truly joys forever!

## Advantages of the Sew-Easy Method

Sew easy offers major advantages that the quickie technique of the sewing machine fails to provide. (The following order of discussion is not an indication of their priority.)

*First, sew easy increases the monetary value of patchwork.* Admittedly, hand sewing requires more time than does machine stitching. This additional time is justified, however, when we consider the fact that the value of the work is increased by 300% or 400%. This, of course, relates to the authenticity of the craft as well as to the quality of construction provided by the gentleness of hand stitching.

Comparing hand-sewn patchwork with that made by machine is like comparing the value and cost of a designer fashion with that of mass-produced, machine-made clothing. Sew easy patchwork has a wonderful potential for supplemental income.

*Second, sew easy is low in cost.* It requires only a minimum of supplies and/or equipment: a needle and thread, a pair of scissors, a thimble, pins, a see-through quilter's ruler and a pencil—and, of course, fabric. It does not require a sewing machine.

*Third, sew easy work is portable and easy to store.* You don't have to sit where the sewing machine sits. You can pick up your patchwork, take it with you, and sit wherever you choose! We have already alluded to storage requirements. They too are minimal.

*Fourth, sew easy provides a way of dealing with stress.* Because sew easy *is* fun and easy and beautiful, even for a first-time patchworker who has never sewn anything, you can lose yourself in the ease of doing it. It lends itself to your interest span, to your time schedule, even to your frame of mind. It never demands a this-must-be-perfect kind of attention. I'm confident that you will begin to look for time to do patchwork.

*And finally, sew easy develops qualities that enrich our lives and those of others through us.* These are the intangibles that I referred to earlier. I cannot argue that the tangibles of patchworking are unimportant as end results. We *can* see and touch them, but, as I have already said, there are other outcomes that *may* be of equal or even greater value in the long run—things we can neither see nor touch, but that are nonetheless real because they *do* touch us and others through us. These are the intangible outcomes that occur naturally when we relate to long-ago homemakers. And *relating* means that we look for and discover differences and similarities in our lives, and further that we grow as individuals in so doing. Relating is unavoidable when we choose to involve ourselves in the doing of an old-fashioned craft like patchwork.

Sew easy is hand stitching, and hand stitching does take time. But this is a decided advantage, because we can *stitch* and *think* and *relate* all at the same time.

When we think about our long-ago counterpart, we think about the sacrifices that were required of her to do patchwork; the taxing demands of her role

as a homemaker, wife, and mother; the resourcefulness and industry she exhibited in gathering together even the barest essentials of patchwork. We begin to see her involvement in the *doing* of patchwork as a representation of her devotion to home and family. We also realize that out of this devotion comes our accessibility to patchwork as a heritage, which in itself carries obligations for safekeeping as a continuing legacy.

Looking at the contrasts in our lives is a humbling experience—it opens our eyes and our hearts. As a result we discover that the following intangibles *do* make a difference:

- While we are filled with gratitude for the comparative ease of our lifestyle, we become keenly aware that a preoccupation with "things" is also easy. We are reminded, however, that the things of enduring value are those of the spirit—things of the heart—those that revolve around home and family, friends and neighbors, people whom we love.

- We develop an appreciation that is heartfelt for the busy homemaker who long ago sacrificed to play with patchwork. Maybe "play" is the wrong word—she was *working* and for an entirely different reason!

- We experience a grateful sense of *belonging* with stronger roots in the past and feelings of obligation to extend them into the future.

- We are challenged by the realization that efforts to perpetuate this beautiful needle skill for generations yet to come is purposeful activity and a significant way to tie past and present and future together.

Now, should you ask me, "Will patchwork continue?" my answer would be an emphatic "Yes!" Why? Because it will always speak of home and family, and certainly of love!

At this point we are ready to look at the *tangibles* of patchwork. We will seek to determine the characteristics of "beautiful" and how we can achieve these in our own efforts to create "joys forever."

# Looking at the
# Qualities of Good Patchwork

## Contrasts in Quality

In today's world we see patchwork literally everywhere. It is still on the beds where it began in an earlier day of America, but now it is found on the walls, on the floors, on the tables, in the chairs, across the sofa, in the kitchen, in the clothes closet—absolutely everywhere. Yes, even on the stuffed goose and the teddy bear!

But when we look closely at some of the tangible end results of today's patchworking, what we really *see* may be neither inspired nor inspiring. As a matter of fact, the old cliché "Patchwork is patchwork" is not applicable here. Patchwork is *not* always patchwork!

First, there is ordinary patchwork—a kind of humdrum collection of scraps of fabrics arranged in a haphazard fashion without regard to color and pattern, lines, shapes, and space. This kind of patchwork merits little or no attention from its *viewer* and very little pride from its *creator*.

But then there is a special kind of patchwork—a beautiful art form that obviously gives attention both to the aesthetics of design as well as skills of workmanship. It is created by an ordered arrange-ment of carefully selected scraps of fabric that are skillfully manipulated to create:

- Patches that fit together
- Design lines that are continuous
- Angles that are sharp and clean
- Seams that lie smooth and flat
- Grainlines that are straight
- Stitches that are neat and even.

In addition, the color and patterns, the lines, shapes and spaces are those that harmoniously blend, that seem to go together, that create a feeling of wholeness in their combination, all of which is patchwork that exhibits the qualities of good design, patchwork that is visually pleasing, patchwork that is truly beautiful.

## What Is Beautiful? (Aesthetic Qualities)

The goal of the sew easy techniques in *Perfect Patchwork* is to make the beautiful kind, the heirlooms-for-the-future kind, the authentic preservation of a heritage needle skill that will be perpetuated through the cycle of viewing and doing for generations yet unborn.

If "beautiful" is the goal you wish to accomplish in your patchworking efforts, it is essential that you understand both aspects of good design: the aesthetics and skills of workmanship. The latter will be discussed at length in chapters 5 and 6. Let's deal with the aesthetics at this point.

Even though "beautiful" is difficult to define or describe precisely, patchwork that is perceived as beautiful possesses certain long-established qualities, which are easily recognized both visually and emotionally. These include: balance, emphasis, scale/proportion, rhythm, and unity. They are discussed below.

*Balance:* Balance is a quality that provides a visual sense of equal weight within patchwork through careful use of color and pattern. Its significance is easily understood when you recall the indescribable joys of childhood derived from balance on a seesaw. You will remember that the seesaw only worked (moved up *and* down) when the weight on either end was almost equal. Likewise, color and pattern carry illusions of weight which, if distributed equally within patchwork, also create balance. When this happens, your patchwork also works—it provides a certain kind of visual satisfaction for every person who sees it. The how-to's of this exciting possibility are presented in Chapter 3.

*Emphasis:* This too is a quality of design, but one that calls attention to a particular element within a given area—a line, a shape, a space. As in the case of balance, emphasis is established within patchwork through the use of *contrast* and *variety* in selection and distribution of color and pattern. I heartily agree with those who say, "When we call attention to everything, we call attention to nothing!" This is just another way of saying that while one element must dominate, all others, though also necessary, must be of secondary importance. Even though a particular element must dominate, it should never diminish the importance of the total design. Thus we recognize that although the quality of emphasis is a necessary provider of visual pleasure within a single block design, it becomes increasingly more important as multiple blocks are joined together to form a larger area of patchwork. The how-to's for this particular quality are also presented in Chapter 3.

*Scale/proportion:* These two design qualities,

usually thought of together, carry similarities of meaning; both terms refer to size relationships, but there are some subtle differences. Scale refers to the comparative size of one whole to another similar whole *or* one whole within another whole; for example, a big chair to a small chair or a big chair in a small room. Proportion refers to the comparative size of one part of a whole to another part of the same whole; for example, the length of a room to the width of the room. The space within a given block design must accommodate the colors and patterns necessary to establish the areas of background, foreground, and accent. The areas of color devoted to each of these functions must be properly scaled to each other. The size of the pattern in fabric must also be scaled to fit within the space (the patch) in which it appears. The proportions of color will be more pleasing if they appear in unequal amounts within the total block design.

*Rhythm:* Rhythm is a quality of design that suggests, as does music, a kind of movement. But in the case of patchwork, it provides a different kind of movement—*a smooth flow of visual interest that moves a viewer from one element to another within a total design and in an organized fashion.* Rhythm is created through the use of color and pattern, and utilizes both variety and contrast (opposites) of tints, shades, tones and/or pattern scale. It is the *arrangement* of these elements that controls the way a viewer actually sees them within the totality of any design. Needless to say, the jumpy, jerky kind of "looking at everything but seeing nothing" tells us immediately that the quality of rhythm is missing! If your patchwork is to be beautiful, the quality of rhythm must exist within single and multiple blocks as they are joined together to form larger areas of patchwork, maybe a quilt for wall, crib, sofa, or bed. The simple how-to's of coloring blocks beautiful, which also means the creation of rhythm, appear in Chapter 3.

*Unity:* Unity is the fifth quality of design that must be present within a given area of patchwork, if the patchwork is to possess the characteristics of beauty. Surely, we can say we have saved the best 'til the last, since this quality encompasses the four that precede and exists only to the degree that the preceding ones also exist within patchwork. Unity refers to a kind of visual agreement or relationship between all of the various elements involved. In other words, when we look at a completed block design, we no longer see it in separate parts—

triangles, squares, and rectangles filled with color and pattern—but rather as an orderly whole, one in which *all* of the various parts seem to go together and appear to have characteristics in common. We create unity when we create the other qualities of beauty, the how-to's of which are presented in Chapter 3. These characteristics are established for patchwork through the use of color, texture or pattern, line, shape and space, just as they are for any other art form.

## A Recipe That Works

The how-to of the process may be more readily understood when we compare it to one with which you may already be more familiar—cake baking, for instance.

For patchwork, as in a recipe for cake baking, there is a list of ingredients (not in precise measurements, however), directions for mixing (also imprecise!), along with a listing of the characteristics that will tell you when beauty is achieved—a kind of test for doneness, in other words!

Let's look at the recipe for *good design* on the accompanying card. One must admit that although the design recipe may be oversimplified, it is a reflection of great great great grandmother's "recipe" for cake baking—a pinch of this, a lump of that, half a handful of something else. But it worked for her a long time ago just as a similar recipe for design will work for you today.

The accuracy of her lump and pinch method of measuring was always verified by looking and tasting. She knew exactly when she needed to add milk, or flour, sugar or butter or any other ingredient that was necessary.

Likewise, the accuracy of your measurements of color, texture, line, shape and space is verified when

---

**GOOD DESIGN**

| Ingredients: | Directions for Mixing: |
|---|---|
| Color | Combine ingredients within any given area of patchwork. Blend together until you *see* and emotionally *feel* the characteristics of balance, emphasis, scale/proportion, rhythm, and unity. |
| Texture | |
| Line | |
| Shape | |
| Space | |

*1. A recipe for good design.*

---

you look at what happens in your patchworking as these ingredients are mixed or blended or put together. You know exactly when the characteristics of balance, emphasis, scale and proportion, rhythm, and unity are achieved; you can *see* them; you can certainly *feel* them; and finally, you know when they are still lacking. Thus, you also know when color, pattern, line, etc., need to be added, rearranged, exchanged, or even removed from your patchwork altogether in order to create good design.

Can we not say then that neither recipe, though seemingly imprecise, is hit or miss nor trial and error? The hit-or-miss methods are frustrating. They consume valuable time, energy, and oftentimes money and are therefore undesirable. The inference of the recipe for good design then is that we learn to do the beautiful kind of patchwork by *doing* patchwork.

Does the recipe for good design work? Oh yes! Indeed it does! This you will discover or experience for yourself when you begin to cut and mark and stitch your way though Chapter 5.

# —3—

# Learning How to Choose:
# Patterns, Fabrics, and Colors

## Introduction

Choice: Privilege! Necessity! Obligation! Most of us fill our days with activity of one kind or another—sometimes routine, sometimes new and different, maybe even sometimes without direction. I assume, however, that the readers of *Perfect Patchwork* involve themselves in purposeful activity, activity with a specific "something" to accomplish: a goal, in other words. While the "something" gives us direction, it also gives us the necessity of choice, moreover, the obligation of *responsible choice*. And this isn't easy! We all know through experience that the wisdom of our choices greatly influences the quality of that which we ultimately accomplish. If our choices are wise, the results are positive. If, on the other hand, our choices are unwise, the outcomes are negative.

But what is the relevance of these statements to a lovely needle skill like patchwork? Let's look at them together. Is it purposeful activity? I would say so! But what about goals? Oh, yes—beautiful in workmanship and design. Choices? Yes, indeed—block design, fabric, color and pattern, tools to work with. Major choices? By all means! And rest assured, they *will* affect the appearance of your patchwork. It will

be beautiful if you choose wisely, just ordinary (or less than) if you make unwise choices. Few of us have time (or the disposition) for trial-and-error choosing. The solution then is one of *learning*—not a comprehensive body of academic knowledge, just some simple, basic information sufficient to make informed choices that will help us increase the loveliness of our patchwork.

As a matter of background necessary for making the named choices wisely, I want to review briefly some facts that are pertinent to each choice, and thus to the tangible outcomes of your patchworking projects as well.

## Definitions of Quilting Terms

In order for you to better understand the terminology used here in the learning chapter, and later in planning and doing, I want us to look at, or listen to, the definition of words used to refer to the components of sew-easy patchwork. A quilt is composed of units of design called *blocks*. The blocks are made up of smaller units, usually *squares*. The squares may be either whole-cloth or pieced. The pieced

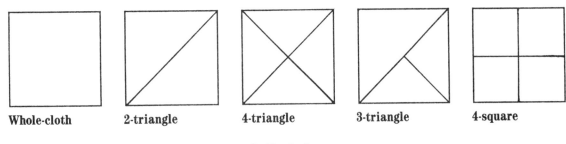

Whole-cloth    2-triangle    4-triangle    3-triangle    4-square

*2. Patch forms.*

squares are formed of *patches*—small geometric shapes that are sewn together in a variety of configurations. The squares are referred to as *square* or *patch forms*. Because the whole-cloth square is actually a one-patch square, the two terms (square form/patch form) are interchangeable! These identified patch forms are illustrated as shown in Figure 2.

## Guidelines for Choosing Block Designs

Our first conscious thought in patchwork is usually one of color rather than one of design. Even so, I suggest we choose the block design first. This is a logical order of choice, since we can't know how many colors are needed nor how they may be effectively distributed within the design until it *is* chosen. In the meantime, let's put your color thoughts in a "think-about" file of ideas. We'll take them out a little later!

The number of block designs from which one may choose is certainly no deterrent to conscientious efforts to preserve authentic patchwork. Quilt historians have indexed literally hundreds of geometric designs, the names of which are fascinating, sometimes quaint and nostalgic, even whimsical, but always picturesque. They paint interesting and revealing word pictures of everyday life in early America, its religious faith, politics, exploration, invention, places and things, plants and animals, routine activities. Some examples: Jacob's Ladder, King's Crown, Clay's Choice, Ohio Star, Tail of Benjamin's Kite, Shoofly, Pine Tree, Puss in the Corner, Churn Dash, Sailing Ships, and the list goes on.

The "joys forever" kind of patchwork, as discussed in Chapter 2, possesses certain visible characteristics that make it beautiful, our goal for patchworking. The ease with which we can achieve this goal is affected by a number of factors present in every block design. They relate to both size and design and include: the finished size of the block, the total number of squares in the design, the finished size of the squares, their patch form or forms, the patch form or forms of adjoining squares, and the total number of patches in the design.

These factors in themselves are neither positive nor negative influences in our efforts to create beautiful patchwork; they can be either, depending on the way we deal with them in construction. *While we cannot choose the factors—the givens of every design—we can choose the way we deal with them!* Because the construction quality of the patch form can determine the overall quality of the completed block design, we need to concentrate on the how-to's of dealing with construction. All the others will then fall into place. Although the factors of size do determine the cutting size of the squares needed to construct the patch forms, they do not directly alter the patchworking process.

I have chosen 24 block designs for *Perfect Patchwork*. Six of the designs will be planned in Chapter 4 and completed in Chapter 5. These are the learning blocks. The eighteen remaining designs will appear as potential heirlooms forever in Chapter 6. The designs incorporate all of the sew-easy skills of construction that ensure the creation of beautiful patchwork. The level of difficulty of the patterns ranges from simple ones, like Nine-Patch, to the complex, like the graphically beautiful Card Tricks, which combines five different fabrics and three different patch forms.

The finished size of each block design presented in the book is 12″ × 12″. This is a good standard size, one that is extremely easy to work with. Having all the blocks the same size also gives you the option of using the six learning blocks in combination with the heirloom designs as a sampler once they are completed—a perfect way to avoid monotony! Nine of the designs have three squares across and down; each square measures 4″ × 4″ when finished (see Table 1). Fifteen of the designs have four squares across and down, each square of which measures 3″ × 3″ when finished. This is a matter of simple math—the finished size of the block divided by the number of squares across equals the finished size of each square (see Table 2).

The 24 designs are listed alphabetically within categories as determined by patch form in Table 3. They are also illustrated in Figure 3 in the same order in line drawings for maximum visibility of squares and patches (p. 20–25). The name of the design, the patch form or forms, and the total number of patches included therein are also noted in Figure 3 for each design. I invite you to examine every single design and very carefully! Later we will do six of them as learning blocks. Each design is potentially beautiful and offers an exciting challenge to our own sense of personal achievement and creativity.

## Skills Needed to Create Beautiful Work

You need to understand the correlation (interdependence) between the characteristics of beautiful patchwork and skills required to make it. The maintenance of accuracy throughout the entire patchworking process serves as a kind of umbrella to the required skills listed in Table 4. These skills are dictated by the patch forms that make up the block design.

Now, I ask you, what exactly does all of the information in Table 4 really say to you? Let's think about that for a moment. Why don't you browse through the block designs again? But look this time for the potential difficulties of making them beautiful: the number of seams that must be matched, those that are bias, those on the straight grain, the color and shapes that change and possibly interrupt the continuity of the design, the thicknesses of fabric that have to be distributed where seams cross, the corners that you must protect from loss within seams that are to be stitched together.

You will discover that beauty is *easier to achieve* in some designs than in others. You will also discover a simple rule of thumb: the more patches, the more seams, and thus the more likelihood of error in

construction. And *that*, you will discover, is the reason for *Perfect Patchwork*, for sew easy, for learning blocks!

While it is important that you be able to *identify* the skills involved in the doing of patchwork, it is essential that you know how to *perform* the skills. The bottom line then is in choosing the way you are going to deal with these skills. Let's look at the ways (techniques of construction) that are open to you.

## Traditional vs. Sew-Easy Methods of Piecing

With traditional methods of patchwork piecing the small geometric shapes—the patches—are cut as such with ¼″ seam allowances added in cutting. Handling these small shapes in each step of construction (measuring, marking, cutting, stitching) is a slow and tedious process that is both frustrating and discouraging to a beginning patchworker. It creates a tremendous margin for error, which is reflected in the appearance of the finished block design. The construction quality of the completed design is therefore dependent on the experience of the patchworker.

In sew-easy construction, all pieced squares begin as whole-cloth squares cut in preplanned colors and sizes that vary according to the patch form you wish to construct (see Table 5). The patch arrangement is drawn directly on one of two paired squares, which are then stitched together *before* they are cut into the small shapes drawn thereon. The resulting patch units ("units" because two squares of fabric have already been sewn together) are color-matched and stitched together to form the squares necessary to make up the total block design.

This particular technique of construction, which I choose to call sew easy because it *is* so easy, can eliminate virtually all of the usual mistakes in patchworking. While sew easy compensates for the lack of experience of the beginner, it also simplifies the entire process for the experienced patchworker. This means that everyone can, in a very literal sense, build blocks without error or frustration. Thus, the promises made at the outset of your reading are fulfilled! Easy! Fun! Beautiful! Just think what this can do for your continuing interest in patchworking and, additionally, for your own self-esteem!

You will be exposed to the details of sew easy in chapters upcoming on planning and doing (Chap-

### Table 1. Block Designs Containing 9 Pieced or Whole-Cloth Squares; Finished Size of Each Square: 4″ × 4″

| | |
|---|---|
| Card Tricks* | Nine-Patch* |
| Clown's Choice | Ohio Star* |
| Helen's Choice | Shoofly |
| Hourglass* | Triplet |
| Jacob's Ladder | |

*Learning blocks.

### Table 2. Block Designs Containing 16 Pieced or Whole-Cloth Squares; Finished Size of Each Square: 3″ × 3″

| | |
|---|---|
| Attic Windows | King's Crown |
| Battlegrounds | Louisiana* |
| Clay's Choice | Old Maid's Puzzle |
| Crosses and Losses | Puss in the Corner |
| Double 4-Patch | Road to Oklahoma |
| Dutchman's Puzzle | Ship |
| Evening Star | Susannah* |
| | Windmill |

*Learning blocks.

### Table 3. The 24 Designs for Doing, Categorized by Patch Form

| Patch Form(s) | Design Name |
|---|---|
| | Nine-Patch |
| | Battlegrounds<br>Dutchman's Puzzle |
| | Attic Windows   Louisiana<br>Clay's Choice   Old Maid's Puzzle<br>Crosses and Losses   Puss in the Corner<br>Double 4-Patch   Road to Oklahoma<br>Evening Star   Ships<br>Helen's Choice   Shoofly<br>King's Crown   Susannah<br>Windmill |
| | Clown's Choice<br>Ohio Star<br>Triplet |
| | Jacob's Ladder |
| | Hourglass |
| | Card Tricks |

ters 5 and 6). Right now, we have some additional choices to make—fabric, color, and pattern, and of course the tools you will need to create beautiful patchwork!

# Fabric

Breathtaking choices: fabric, color, pattern! You are already aware that fabric serves as a medium for the doing of patchwork, one through which we introduce color and pattern. These two influential ingredients can (with careful selection) cause your block designs to come alive with exciting dimensions of character that reflect your personality.

The fabrics we choose relate directly to several matters previously discussed. They are listed for your review:

- The goal for sew easy—patchwork that is beautiful in both workmanship and design
- The visible characteristics of beautiful patchwork
- The doing skills required to achieve each characteristic
- The selection of learning blocks designed to teach these identified skills.

When you pull the various topics together in your own mind, I think you will conclude immediately that the fabrics you choose *do* determine, in large measure, the overall quality of your patchwork. Understanding the whys of this relationship—fabric choice and patchwork quality—influences the development of your patchworking skills and, in like manner, your pleasure in performing them successfully. But we will get into this momentarily.

In the usual choosing of fabric, we are simultaneously choosing color and pattern as well. For the sake of a more meaningful discussion, however, I want to separate them here and talk about fabric as such—how it affects the skills of workmanship, about color and pattern as they relate to the aesthetics of design. You will put color and pattern back together when you actually choose in the store those fabrics that will ultimately be, as some describe them, "a delight to the senses."

I am assuming that I have some readers who are beginning patchworkers, with little knowledge of fabric usage. Obviously, they have special learning needs which must be addressed, so bear with me, if you are an experienced patchworker, as we review some basic information. Any repetition of comments

## Table 4.  Characteristics of Beautiful Patchwork and Skills Required

| Characteristics | Skills Required |
|---|---|
| Patches and/or squares that fit together without visible evidence of error, neither fullness nor stretch. | Careful handling of bias seams within pieced squares to maintain sizes dictated by the block design. |
| Design lines that are continuous and without interruption as colors and shapes change. | Precise matching of all converging seams: horizontal, vertical, *and* diagonal (bias). |
| Angles that are sharp and clean. | Proper manipulation of all converging seams that form 45° angles. |
| Seamlines that are smooth and flat with no lumps or bumps on the top surface. | Establishment of an order of directional turn for seam allowances at all points of convergence. (Count the seams, multiply by two and you know how many fabric thicknesses you must deal with). |
| Squares and/or blocks that lie flat and square without twisting or wrinkling. | Establishment of straight grainlines as beginning squares are measured and cut. |
| Seamlines that are strong and durable, smooth and flat. | Uniformity of stitch length and careful selection of needle sizes (and a little experience!) |

## Table 5. Guide to Patch Form and Cutting Size

All pieced squares in sew-easy construction begin as *whole-cloth squares* that are cut to include seam allowances for the patch form you will construct. The cutting sizes are indicated below.

| Patch Form | Cutting Size for Whole-Cloth Squares | Appears in Designs |
|---|---|---|
| Whole-cloth | Finished size of square plus ½″ | Nine-Patch,* Hourglass,* Ohio Star,* Susannah,* Louisiana,* Attic Windows, Clay's Choice, Clown's Choice, Evening Star, Crosses and Losses, Double 4-Patch, Helen's Choice, King's Crown, Old Maid's Puzzle, Puss in the Corner, Road to Oklahoma, Ship, Shoofly, Triplet, Windmill |
| 2-triangle | Finished size of pieced square plus ⅞″ (cut one square for each color appearing herein) | Hourglass,* Susannah,* Louisiana,* Card Tricks,* Attic Windows, Battlegrounds, Clay's Choice, Dutchman's Puzzle, Crosses and Losses, Double 4-Patch, Evening Star, Helen's Choice, Jacob's Ladder, King's Crown, Old Maid's Puzzle, Puss in the Corner, Road to Oklahoma, Ships, Shoofly, Windmill |
| 4-triangle | Finished size of pieced square plus 1⅜″ (cut one square for each color appearing herein) | Ohio Star,* Card Tricks,* Clown's Choice, Triplet |
| 3-triangle | Finished size of pieced square plus ⅞″ for the 1-triangle half; finished size of square plus 1⅜″ for the 2-triangle half (cut one square for each color appearing herein) | Card Tricks* |
| 4-square | Cut two rectangles (2½″ × 5″) for each color appearing herein | Hourglass,* Jacob's Ladder |

*Learning blocks.

with which you are already familiar may be of benefit, nonetheless.

Understanding the *why* of any action makes the doing of that action much easier and far more productive. A case in point—choosing fabric that will maximize the quality of patchwork while minimizing the difficulty of the *doing* skills, a sew-easy kind of doing!

The various aspects of the structuring of fabric—the fibre and the way it is put together—determine how a fabric will look, how it will feel, how it will behave, and how it must be cared for. Some general

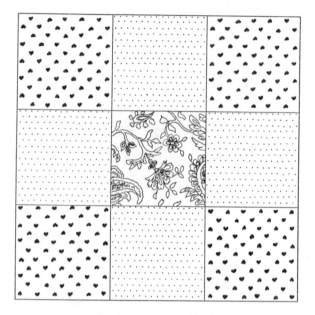

**Nine-Patch: 9 patches**

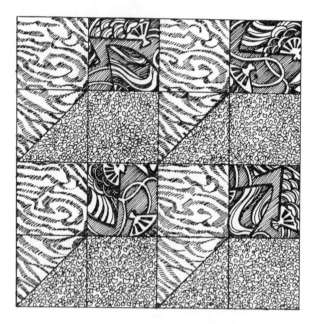

**Attic Windows: 20 patches**

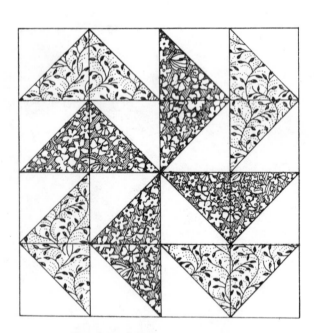

**Dutchman's Puzzle: 32 patches**

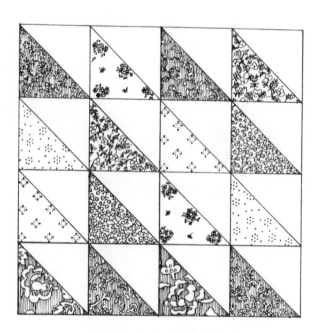

**Battlegrounds: 32 patches**

*3. Diagrams of the 24 patchwork designs for doing and the patch forms used to make them.*

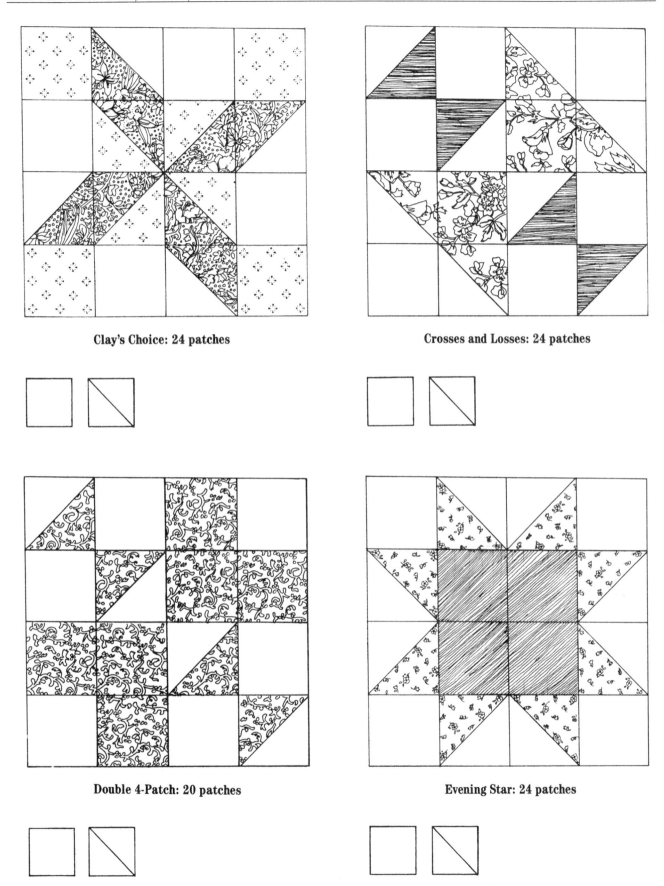

Clay's Choice: 24 patches

Crosses and Losses: 24 patches

Double 4-Patch: 20 patches

Evening Star: 24 patches

*3. Diagrams of the 24 patchwork designs, continued*

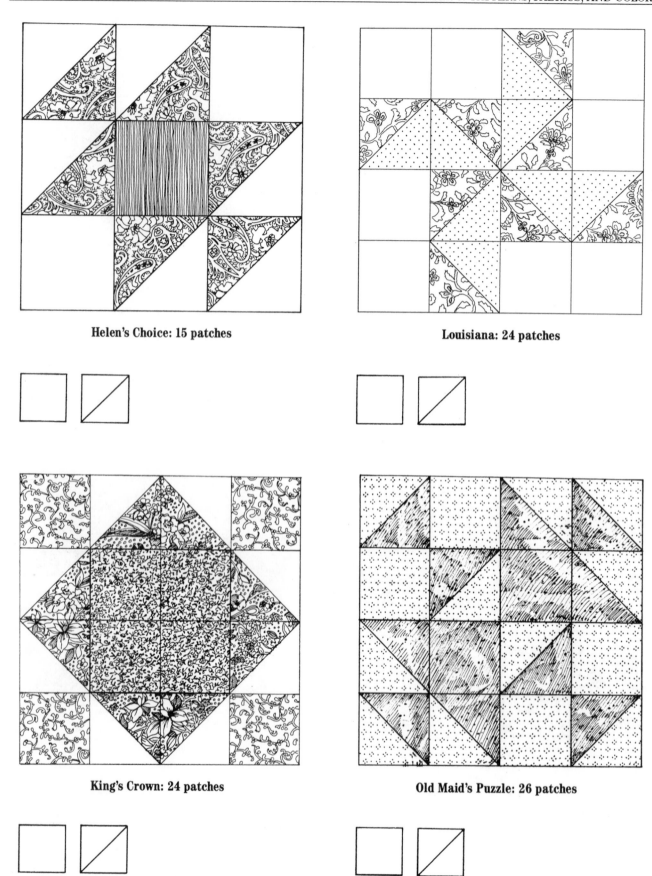

Helen's Choice: 15 patches

Louisiana: 24 patches

King's Crown: 24 patches

Old Maid's Puzzle: 26 patches

3. *Diagrams of the 24 patchwork designs, continued*

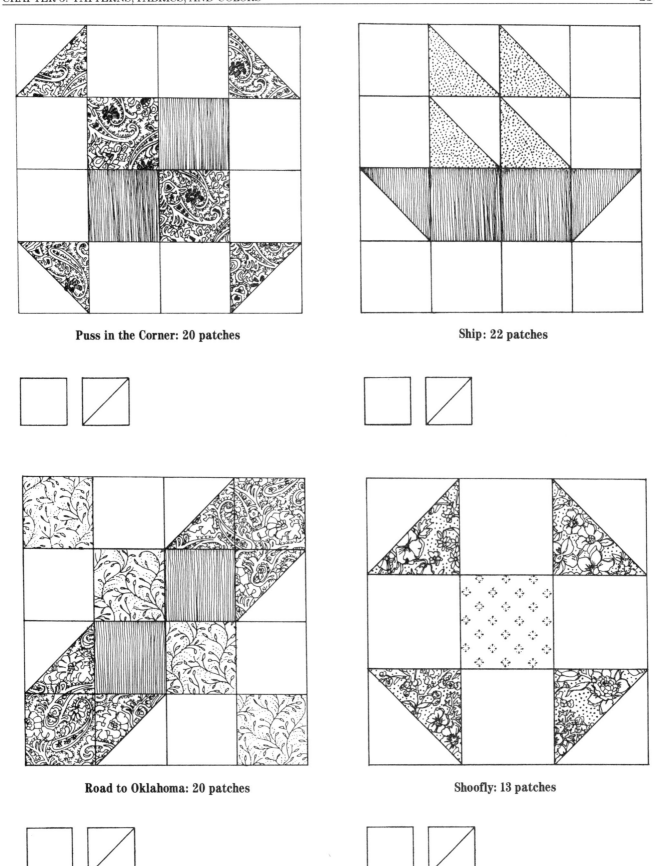

Puss in the Corner: 20 patches

Ship: 22 patches

Road to Oklahoma: 20 patches

Shoofly: 13 patches

*3. Diagrams of the 24 patchwork designs, continued*

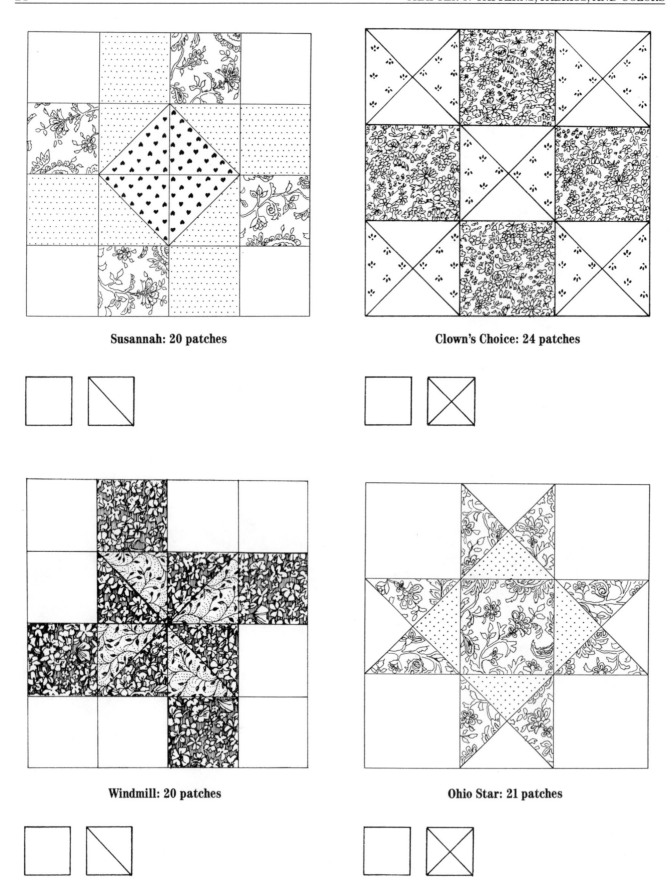

3. *Diagrams of the 24 patchwork designs, continued*

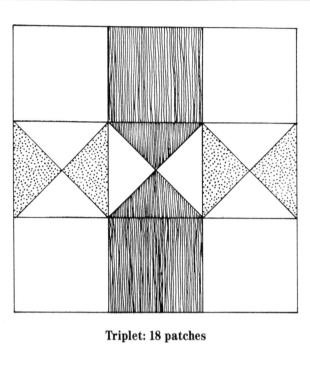

**Triplet: 18 patches**

**Hourglass: 14 patches**

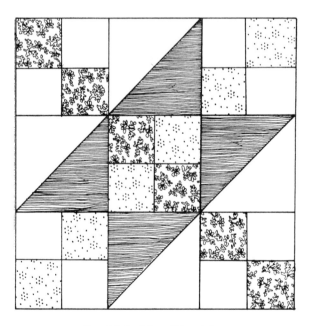

**Jacob's Ladder: 28 patches**

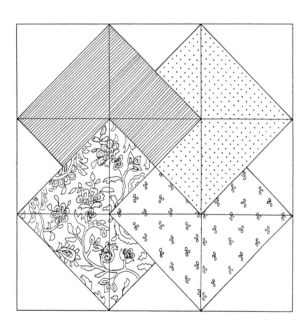

**Card Tricks: 24 patches**

*3. Diagrams of the 24 patchwork designs, continued*

understanding of the construction process can therefore explain the relationship between fabric choice and patchwork quality.

## Fabric Terms You Need to Know

In the interest of brevity I offer some definitions of terms designed to provide the *why* answers. The expanding comments are introduced to help you associate the terms as defined with sew-easy patchwork, so think about them in that light as you move through the comments. See Figure 4 also.

*Fibre:* A fabric-making ingredient, classified according to its origin as either natural or manmade.
- Every fibre has distinct characteristics of appearance, comfort, behavior, and care requirements.
- These characteristics are never lost or destroyed, but are transmitted through the weaving process to the fabric in which the fibre appears. They may, however, be altered in finishing to compensate for any disadvantages, for a specific end use. For example, some fabrics have a tendency to wrinkle easily. While wrinkle-resistance may be of little consequence for general end use, it may be of extreme importance for others. This characteristic can therefore be offset with special finishes applied during the manufacturing process, thus making the fabric wrinkle-resistant.
- Fibres are sometimes blended together to produce a fabric that also minimizes any disadvantage of the fibres in question. You must remember, however, that the characteristics of fibre are always retained. So instead of having to deal with those of only *one* fibre, you must deal with the characteristics of *two* or even *three* fibres in a blended fabric. And though you may gain a desirable characteristic, you risk the potential gain of undesirable ones as well. In other words, fabric blends involve a tradeoff in an effort to satisfy the major requirements of a particular end use.

*Weave:* The structure of fabric, which begins with the conversion of fibre into yarn, progressing to yarn into thread, and finally thread into cloth.
- Fibres are spun into yarn. Plies or strands of yarn are combined to produce thread, which is then woven into cloth. The number and form of the plies affect the texture, weight, beauty and comfort of the finished fabric. (The terms *yarn* and *thread* are often used interchangeably.)

- The basic process of weaving involves two sets of yarns (vertical and horizontal), which cross each other at right angles. This is known as a *plain weave*; it is the simplest or most common in use. Both threads run alternately over one, under one, thus forming a surface that is smooth to the touch.
- The plain-weave fabrics with which we are more familiar are calico, percale, muslin, gingham, chambray, and other shirting type fabrics.

*Selvage:* The crosswise thread runs continuously across the fabric. The "turnaround" areas formed at both vertical edges of the fabric are known as the *selvages*.
- The selvage is closely woven, very strong and stable, and therefore difficult to manipulate in hand stitching.
- Because the selvage has a tendency to "draw" in any construction, it must be trimmed away before the fabric is used.

*Grain:* A quality that is inherent to the construction of fabric (regardless of fibre content); it has to do with the reaction of fabric to the various techniques of a given end-use construction. The word *grain* is also used to refer to the direction in which the yarns run to create the fabric.

*Straight Grain:* The right-angle crossing of the lengthwise and crosswise yarns in the weaving of the fabric.
- Any distortion of grain usually occurs in the finishing stages following the weaving process.
- The grain must be straightened if necessary before a fabric is used (see p. 93). This may be resisted by some fabrics.

*Lengthwise Grain:* The direction of yarns that run parallel to the selvage edges of fabrics.
- Because the lengthwise thread is subjected to the greater amount of wear in the weaving process, it is the stronger, more stable of the two threads.
- The lengthwise grain has *no* flexibility and as a consequence is difficult to manipulate in stitching.

*Crosswise Grain:* The direction of yarns that run continuously across the fabric from one selvage to the other, and at right angles to the lengthwise yarns.
- This grain has some flexibility and is therefore easier to manipulate than is the lengthwise grain.

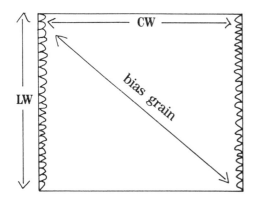

*4. Diagram of fabric, showing lengthwise grain (LW), crosswise grain (CW), bias grain, and selvage.*

*Bias Grain:* Any diagonal intersection of the right-angle crossing of the lengthwise and crosswise yarns.

- A true bias (one that forms a 45°-intersection) is established by folding an on-grain fabric so that the lengthwise and crosswise yarns are parallel to each other.
- The bias grain has a maximum of stretch and must be handled with extreme care when piecing triangular patches together to form squares and blocks so that they actually *are* square after piecing.

Each of the terms defined and illustrated is significant to patchwork quality and will therefore serve as a helpful reference when we move into doing in Chapter 5.

But for the here and now, the information on fabric structure we just discussed has implications for positive choice-making: a recognition of the decisive characteristics of fabric for patchworking—those that are needed, those that are wanted, those that are provided! Let's examine all three. First, those we need (Table 6), those that relate to the demands or techniques of sew-easy.

The second listing we should look at is that of the *wanted* characteristics, those that are relevant to general home sewing. This list is easy to compile when we think about characteristics as stipulated in our earlier discussion—how we want our fabric to look, to feel, to behave, to be cared for. The list below is *my* list. If you have other characteristics you wish to add, or maybe just to express in a different way, please feel free to do so, but *do not delete* a single one of these!

- Closely woven
- Medium weight
- Smooth-textured
- Strong- and long-wearing
- Free from static buildup
- Soft and comfortable to touch
- Resistant to pilling (surface balls)
- Washable
- Shrink resistant
- Colorfast
- Gives up soil and stain easily
- Insensitive to hot water, strong detergents, bleaches
- Dimensionally stable (doesn't stretch)
- Available in traditional colors and patterns

## Table 6.  Sew-Easy Techniques and Fabric Characteristics Needed

| Techniques of Sew-Easy | Needed Fabric Characteristics |
| --- | --- |
| • Hand stitching | • Easy manipulation in hand sewing (needling and distribution of fullness) |
| • Establishment of a straight crosswise grain | • Tears easily on the crosswise grain |
| • Finger-pressing of seams for a smooth upper surface, as well as ease of assembly and quilting | • Responsive to creasing by hand |
| • ¼″ seam allowances | • Resistant to ravelling |
| • Grain perfect squares and blocks | • Responsive to correction of grain distortion; maintains straight of grain |

Let's look at a listing of the inherent characteristics for the two fibres commonly used in home sewing, cotton and polyester (Table 7).

A careful review of the inherent characteristics tells us that both cotton and polyester offer advantages and disadvantages for general use in home sewing. Since it is the *disadvantages* that present potential difficulties, I have listed them for yet another look in Table 8.

As we continue to think about these inherent characteristics and how they relate to both those that are needed for sew easy and those that are wanted for comfort, convenience, and long wear, we learn some surprising facts. First, cotton provides every single one of the five needed characteristics, every one of the fourteen wanted characteristics; furthermore, the four disadvantages of cotton are of little consequence to patchworking. They can be easily overcome through wise shopping and proper care. On the other hand, polyester provides none of the needed characteristics, and only six of the fourteen wanted characteristics. *None* of the seven disadvantages of polyester can be overcome for patchworking.

Surely we can agree with uncounted numbers of experienced teachers and doers of patchwork alike, that the fabric of choice for this lovely needle skill is *100% cotton!*

# Color

## Choosing Colors and Patterns

Color blocks beautiful! We have already learned how to choose the fabric base; we must now build blocks that exhibit the exciting dimensions of character and personality discussed earlier. Coloring blocks beautiful, adding pattern for personality—*your* personality, *your* block design and never a copy of one that belongs to someone else—is the task of immediate concern.

Very few people have an instinctive flair for effective use of color and pattern. Fortunately, however, this *is* a skill that can be learned. In fact, choosing these two design ingredients can be a fun-time task, an easy task, a "learn-to-choose-by-choosing" task. If you are to accomplish this kind of choice-making, there are a few fundamentals of both theory and practice that must be learned—those that provide the *why* answers for the practicality of choosing colors and patterns that create *beautiful* patchwork, patchwork that incorporates all of the principles of good design discussed in Chapter 2. The learning requirements that have to do with color theory include:

- The dimensions (properties or qualities) of color
- The basic structure or relationships of colors, as depicted by the color wheel (see figures 5, 6, and 7).
- Established patterns for pleasing combinations of color—those that "go together" successfully.

The learning requirements that have to do with the practical aspects of choosing color and pattern include:

- The procedures involved in the selection and distribution of color and pattern for your learning blocks
- The procedures involved in the evaluation of color and pattern, selection and distribution, for your learning blocks
- A visual summary of the do's and do nots for choosing color and pattern—a review of choices for the learning blocks
- The pretreatment of fabric to eliminate any potential hindrance to the creation of beautiful patchwork.

Once you get to this point, you are ready to move into the planning and doing chapters. Complicated? Not if you concentrate on one fundamental at a time, closing out the distractions of all others.

## Color Terms You Need to Know

I have chosen to repeat the definitions-of-terms approach that we used earlier to acquaint you with the *why* answers for choosing fabric. Let's look at the terms related to color; the expanding comments are designed to help you make positive choices of color and pattern.

*Dimensions of Color:* the measurements, properties, or qualities of any given color appearing on the color wheel. These qualities are hue, value, and intensity.

*Hue:* The name of the color as it appears on the color wheel. Red, yellow, blue, green and orange are hues; there are twelve of them.

## Table 7. Characteristics of Cotton and Polyester, Compared

| Cotton | Polyester |
|---|---|
| • Easy to manipulate in both hand sewing and machine sewing | • Difficult to manipulate in hand sewing (springy nature of fibre makes needling difficult, holding-in of fullness impossible!) |
| • Washable—insensitive to water, detergents, bleaches | • Wash-and-wear—sensitive to heat, strong detergents, chlorine bleach |
| • Excellent soil release and stain release | • Affinity for oily stains |
| • Strong and durable | • High strength |
| • Not susceptible to pilling or seam slippage | • Susceptible to both pilling and seam slippage |
| • Tears easily, ravels very little | • Difficult to tear, ravels easily |
| • Tendency to wrinkle unless treated | • Excellent wrinkle resistance and abrasion resistance |
| • Responsive to creasing by hand | • Retains heat-set creases only |
| • Comfortable, absorbent, carries heat away from the body | • Hard-surfaced, low absorbency, holds in body heat |
| • Free from static buildup | • Accumulates static electricity and surface lint |
| • Good affinity for dyes, colorfast if treated | • May yellow, otherwise colorfast |
| • Tendency to shrink if untreated | • Resistant to shrinkage |
| • Will deteriorate from mildew or strong sunlight | • Excellent resistance to mildew |

## Table 8. Disadvantages of Cotton and Polyester

| Cotton | Polyester |
|---|---|
| • Tendency to wrinkle | • Springy nature of fibre makes manipulation by hand extremely difficult, holding-in of fullness impossible |
| • Will shrink if untreated | • Resistant to tearing |
| • Weakened by strong sunlight | • Ravels easily |
| • Subject to mildew | • Surface pilling |
| | • Possesses an affinity for oily stains |
| | • Hard-surfaced, uncomfortable to the touch |
| | • Sensitive to hot water, strong detergents, chlorine bleach |

• Six of the twelve hues, those containing either yellow or red, are classified as *warm colors*. The six that contain blue or green are classified as *cool colors*.

• Names like barn red, country blue, daffodil, spring green, wild cherry, periwinkle, and shocking pink are chosen by various manufacturers and/or tradespeople to market the goods they produce—selling tools, in other words. These names, arbitrarily chosen by the manufacturer, are imprecise descriptions of color. They represent whatever a particular manufacturer wishes them to represent.

*Value:* Value refers to the lightness or darkness of a given color on the color wheel.

- If white is added, the color becomes lighter and is referred to as a *tint* of the original hue.
- If black is added, the color becomes darker and is referred to as a *shade* of the original hue.

*Intensity:* Intensity refers to the brightness or dullness of a color as it appears on the color wheel.

- The intensity of a color is dulled by adding either gray or the complement of the color in question. The resulting color is then called a *tone* of the original hue.
- The opposite effect of dulling is created, however, when two complements in actual fabric are used side by side: both fabric colors appear much brighter.
- The complement of a given color is the color that is directly opposite it on the color wheel.

## The Color Wheel

The color wheel (Fig. 5) is an organization of colors that is designed to depict their basic structure or relationship to each other. The twelve colors appearing thereon are divided into three groups—primary colors, secondary colors, and tertiary colors—according to their order of formation (see Fig. 6).

- The primaries are red, yellow, and blue. All other colors are formed from these three *base colors.*
- The secondaries, also three in number, are formed by mixing two primaries together. Red and yellow make orange, yellow and blue make green, blue and red make purple.
- In like manner, the tertiaries are formed when two adjacent hues, a primary and a secondary, are mixed together. There are six tertiary colors. For example, yellow and orange make yellow-orange, orange and red make red-orange, red and purple make red-purple, and so on around the wheel.
- One of the major difficulties for a beginning patchworker is the identity or placement of the various tints, shades, and tones of color in actual fabric, within what I call "the family from whence they came." This takes some conscious looking for colors within colors. But they are easy to see if you really look for them! Try doing this from where you sit at this moment.
- This *identity with a color family* is a necessary

first step to effective use of the color wheel as a source for choosing color harmonies that really work in patchwork piecing.

- Black, white and gray are without hue or color and are referred to as *neutrals.* They may be used in any harmony without disruption.

## Patterns of Color Harmonies

Pleasing combinations of color can be developed by following the established principles of color use as depicted by the color wheel. These harmonies, as they are called, include monochromatic colors, related or analogous colors, and complementary colors.

*Monochromatic Harmony:* A monochromatic color combination utilizes tints, shades, and/or tones of *one* color—any color. It is a restful, quieting combination, extremely easy to create, therefore perfect for beginning patchworkers.

- The addition of textural interest in the form of pattern is often necessary to avoid monotony.

*Related or Analogous Harmony:* A related or analogous color harmony combines two or more colors that are adjacent to each other on the color wheel.

- A related color harmony also creates a feeling of peacefulness, which may be due to the fact that you are placing relatives together—they share colors in common. This gives you the option of using two, three or more colors successfully. Three colors, however, work well in most of the sew-easy designs.

*Triadic Harmony:* A triadic harmony involves any three colors that are equally spaced on the color wheel, the most popular of which is a combination of the primaries—red, blue, and yellow. But again, a triadic harmony requires a variety of color values and/or intensities for successful use. The triads are traditional in feeling and extremely easy to formulate.

*Complementary Harmony:* A complementary color harmony, as is implied by the name itself, is a combination of opposites, of contrasts—warm colors and cool colors. It is lively and exciting. A complementary harmony requires variations in both value and intensity for successful use, which many doers of patchwork find difficult to formulate.

5. *The color wheel.*

• There are three different complementary combinations from which you may choose: the *direct* complement, the *split* complement, and the *double* complement. Some are more difficult than others.

*Direct Complementary Harmony:* The direct complementary harmony involves two colors that are directly opposite each other on the color wheel: one cool color and one warm color.

*Split Complementary Harmony:* The split complementary harmony utilizes three colors: one color plus the two colors adjacent to its complement. The split complementary harmony serves as a kind of transition between warm and cool, therefore it is somewhat less difficult to use than the direct complementary harmony.

*Double Complementary Harmony:* The double complementary harmony combines four colors: two adjacent colors plus both of their complements. This is a challenging combination for most patchworkers, one that is seldom chosen because of the limitations imposed by the design of the block itself.

Successful combinations! They are (or soon will be) *just* that! But at this point, they have to be translated into tints, tones, and shades of color within actual fabric before they become a part of beautiful patchwork. Figures 5, 6 and 7 will serve as

choosing tools to help you color your blocks beautiful. The Personal Harmony Chart (Table 9) is provided for your use in identifying the color wheel colors in each of the six color harmony patterns that are compatible with a beginning color of your choosing. Each harmony pattern is described in the column on the left. The color of choice (beginning color) appears in the center column. The additional colors suggested for harmonious combinations are recorded in the column on the right. Red is used as the example in the form as illustrated. (A blank copy of this form appears in the Appendix for your use.)

Whenever we choose a block design, we also choose certain "givens" of line, shape and space.

## Perception of Color

The preceding study of color fundamentals—dimensions or measurements, relationships, and patterns for successful combinations—is more than *just* theory. Actually it has some subtle implications for the practical use of color and pattern to create good design, defined in Chapter 2.

When we examine these implications carefully, we discover that the variations within each dimension of color create visual perception of size, weight, and temperature, which can be used to advantage in our choice-making. In other words, the qualities of beautiful patchwork, created through the use of

PRIMARY

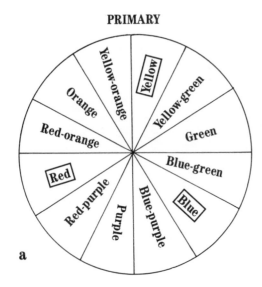

a

TERTIARY

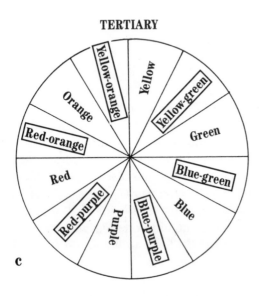

c

SECONDARY

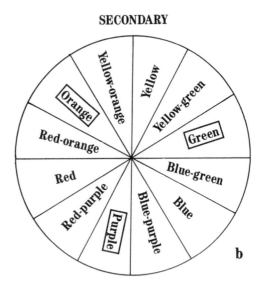

b

*6. Categories of colors. a: Primary. b: Secondary. c: Tertiary.*

Table 10 tells us how the variations of the color wheel colors will look in a block design *before the fabric is purchased* or stitched into your learning blocks. The dimensions of color appear in the column on the left. The variations that are perceived or seen as larger, heavier and more visible appear in the center column. The variations in the right-hand column are perceived as smaller, lighter in weight and less visible as is so indicated. These variance perceptions serve as choosing guides and are used to create the qualities of beautiful as defined in Chapter 2.

## Procedural Outline for Choosing Colors and Patterns

May I offer now (in chronological order) an outline or listing of procedural activities involved in the choosing of color and pattern? This is the sixth tool for choosing colors successfully. I must say here at the outset that pattern *is* color—*what* color it is can be more easily determined from a distance, but it must be determined if you are to use color and pattern successfully.

*First, do some reflective thinking.* Think about some of the facts that have special significance to this exciting task of choosing color and pattern.

color and pattern, come about as a result of variance perceptions—the way we *see* color.

Remember, though, that the colors, as they appear on the color wheel, are pure colors and, as such, are far too strong for satisfactory use in patchwork. They simply represent the *color family* to which the tints, tones, and shades in actual fabric belong.

The color perception chart (Table 10) is designed to clarify the how-to's necessary to choose *and* distribute the "just right" variations of any color as it appears on the color wheel, and in any of the color harmonies outlined earlier. Study the perceptions chart carefully. It serves as the fifth tool for choosing and using colors successfully.

**ANALOGOUS**

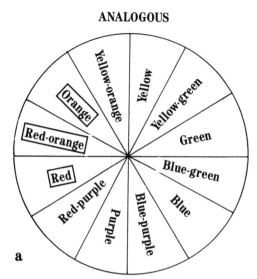

a

**TRIADIC**

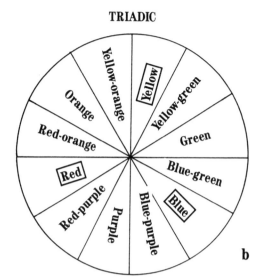

b

**DIRECT COMPLEMENT**

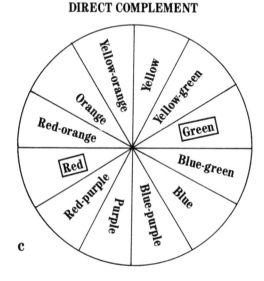

c

**SPLIT COMPLEMENT**

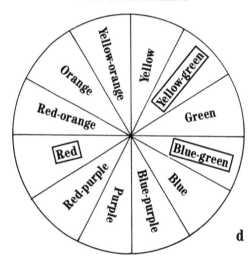

d

**DOUBLE COMPLEMENT**

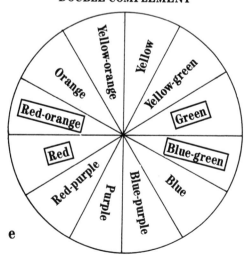

e

**MONOCHROMATIC**

+ white    ← hue →    + black

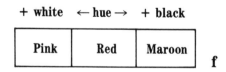

| Pink | Red | Maroon |

f

7. *Patterns for harmonious color combinations, using red as the starting hue. a, Analogous. b, Triadic. c, Direct complement. d, Split complement. e, Double complement. f, Monochromatic.*

## Table 9.  Personal Harmony Chart

This is an example of various color harmonies starting with the red hue. The same could be done for any hue.

| Name of Color Harmony | Beginning Color | Additional Colors for Blending |
|---|---|---|
| **MONOCHROMATIC** Uses tints, shades, and tones of one color— any color. Pattern is added to avoid monotony. | Red | Pink, rose, maroon |
| **ANALOGOUS OR RELATED** Made of two or more colors adjacent to each other on the color wheel. | Red | Red-orange, orange, yellow-orange *or* red-purple, purple, blue-purple |
| **TRIADIC** Made of any three colors that are equidistant on the color wheel. | Red | Yellow, blue |
| **DIRECT COMPLEMENT** Two colors that are directly opposite each other on the color wheel are direct complements. | Red | Green |
| **SPLIT COMPLEMENT** One color plus two colors next to its complement create a split complement. | Red | Yellow-green, blue-green |
| **DOUBLE COMPLEMENT** Two adjacent colors plus both their complements together create a double complement | Red | Red-orange, green, blue-green *or* red-purple, green, yellow-green |

## Table 10.  Color Perception Chart

| Dimensions or Measurements of Color | Range of Variances | |
|---|---|---|
| Hue | Warm | Cool |
| Value | Dark | Light |
| Intensity | Bright | Dull |
| Variance Perceptions Created | Warm, dark, bright: heavy weight, large size, more visible | Cool, light, dull: lighter weight, smaller size, less visible |

- Our job as *doers* of patchwork is to catch the attention of the *viewers*, and thus to encourage them to look more closely at the beauty of a total design (both workmanship and design aesthetics). Hopefully, viewers are thereby moved into the status of doers! This is our *only assurance* that patchwork will continue for the infinite pleasure of people everywhere—even for those yet to come!

- Color and pattern perform many functions within patchwork. They can increase or decrease the size of shapes and spaces, call attention to the important elements of a total design, delineate areas within the block design (background, foreground, accent) and tie all the elements together to form a pleasing whole. They can also create a mood or atmosphere, reflect your personality, and provide a special kind of personal satisfaction that is extremely important to every single individual.

- These functions actually represent the characteristics or qualities we are seeking to establish within sew-easy patchwork.
- The beauty of a total design is measured in terms of your attainment of the qualities of beautiful—balance, emphasis, scale and proportion, rhythm, unity. (These qualities were defined in Chapter 2.)
- The qualities of beautiful created through the use of color and pattern come about as a result of the variance perceptions—the way we see color. Go back now and *reread* the definitions of beautiful in Chapter 2, in order to clarify *exactly* what it is you are trying to do with color and pattern.
- Remember too, that harmonious colors cost no more than do those that clash with each other; besides, they provide tremendous dividends in personal satisfaction!

*Second, begin the formulation of a list of colors that you wish to consider for your learning blocks.*

- Start by rethinking the color ideas you put in a "think-about" file during the discussions for choosing block designs earlier. Take all your ideas out again. Add or delete any color you wish, then list three or four colors you *really* like or *think* you like! I call this kind of list my *want list* of colors.
- With the want list in hand (or head), think about any relevant factors of use that might influence your final choices. The following questions may stimulate your thinking. *How* do you plan to use the completed designs? As a framed wall-hanging? A pillow? The beginning blocks for a sampler collection? *Where* do you plan to use them? To *whom* will they be given? Will they be used as single blocks or in multiples? *Which* mood or atmosphere do you wish to create? *What* are the colors around which you must work—the existing colors that must be retained?
- You are in a position at this point to make a second list of colors based on your response to these questions. These are the colors you *need*. I call such a list my "must-have" list of colors and they usually take priority over the colors I like.
- Once you are satisfied with the list of must-have

colors, combine the two lists—those you want *and* those you need or "must have."

- Place them in order of priority, with your favorite-of-favorites at the top of the list. Now designate the *one* color that will serve as your key color. This color will be used to select the color harmony for your learning blocks.

*Third, reacquaint yourself with three of the decisive choosing tools that will guide you through a process of positive choice-making.*

- These three tools (the color wheel, the patterns for harmonious color combinations, and the Personal Harmony Chart, figures 5–7 and Table 9) will help you translate color theory into practical, easy to understand how-to's for choosing.
- The twelve colors appearing on the color wheel are pure colors and, as such, are too strong for your use in patchwork.
- Actually the twelve colors represent families of color that have countless variations—tints, shades, tones, and temperatures—that *are* used in patchwork.
- Your ability to identify the family to which a color in actual fabric belongs is a necessary first step to the successful use of color wheel patterns for combining colors. This ability is developed through a thoughtful study of color variations between fabrics when they are *placed together* for observation. And of course, experience is a wonderful teacher.
- There are six color harmony patterns from which you may choose: the monochromatic, analogous or related, triadic, direct complement, split complement, and double complement. You will feel much more comfortable using these patterns if you are knowledgeable about the details of their formulation. So go back and examine both their descriptions and illustrations earlier in this chapter.
- The Personal Harmony Chart (Table 9) is provided to help you identify the color wheel colors in each of the six color harmonies that are compatible with the key color of your choosing. As you look at the example in Table 9, you will see that each harmony is described in the left-hand column. The additional colors suggested for harmonious combinations appear in the right column. The color *red* is used as the key color in the illustration, but any color could be used. A blank copy of

the Personal Harmony Chart appears in the Appendix for your use.

*Fourth, identify all of the colors that may be successfully combined with those on your want and need or must-have list of colors:*

- Using the color wheel, the illustrated example of the Personal Harmony Chart (Table 9), and your own key color, complete your own Personal Harmony Chart.

- When you have done this, transfer the lists of colors (by harmonies) to separate index cards for easy reference in your upcoming shopping activities. The cards will also make wonderful keepsake records of your first efforts in sew-easy patchworking; for some people they may be the first efforts in patchworking.

- Compare the colors in these individual harmonies with those on your want and need lists. Choose two or three of the combinations that include the want and need colors that you feel you simply cannot give up. These colors then become your "shopping" colors. But hold onto your harmony chart and the cards. You may change your mind!

*Fifth, walk through an overview of the how-to's for choosing color and pattern.* These how-to's actually represent the application of important design principles, so I want to begin with a few observations. Rules sometimes simplify the doing of an activity. But with color, there are *no* absolutes and therefore *no* rules—just some long-established *principles of design*. And principles require judgments—yours! Though it need not be, this is somewhat intimidating for beginning patchworkers. Rules take away exciting privileges—decision-making, individuality of choice, personal creativity! But we retain all of these with principles, so I like them. You will too! The how-to's are easy to follow if you look and listen. The visual examples of these principles in use, which are found in the color insert of this book, will reinforce the verbal how-to's. The order of presentation that follows relates to the qualities of good design (beautiful) and follows the sequence of their discussion in Chapter 2. Go back and read the definitions again.

- Color variations carry illusions of weight and size that can either enhance or disturb the beauty of a total block design. The effects created by these variances are presented in the Color Perception Chart (Table 10). I strongly recommend that you

become completely familiar with the information contained therein. It is the basis for all of the how-to's for choosing color and pattern. So read this with care.

- Let's begin now with the quality of *balance*. It is established through an *equal* distribution of weight and size. And according to the Color Perception Chart, the warm colors, darker shades and brighter tones appear heavier, larger, and more conspicuous. This means that a small area of a warm color will balance a larger area of a cool color; a small area of a darker shade or value will balance a larger area of a lighter shade or value; a small area of an intense or bright color will balance a larger area of a muted or dulled color.

- The second aesthetic quality, that of emphasis, is also essential to the creation of beautiful patchwork. Emphasis has two basic ingredients: variety and contrast. Both must be incorporated into your patchwork. *Variety*, a lack of sameness, requires that you include different colors and different shades, tints, and tones. *Contrast* requires that some of the differing elements be opposites. For example: warm/cool, light/dark, muted or dull/bright, straight lines/curved lines, patterns/solids. Complements also are opposites: blue/orange, yellow/purple, red/green, for example. Remember that too much of either ingredient is just as detrimental to appearance as too little.

- Choose a color for emphasis and then allow this key color to dominate within the shapes, spaces or lines of the design.

- You *may* have more than one element of interest, but *only one can dominate*. Even so, it must never, ever overpower the rest of the design.

- Many patchwork designs require a minimum of three different colors: a background, a foreground, an accent color.

- The background color uses up the largest area of space. It should, therefore, be neutral in color (a solid or an all-over pattern that gives the effect of a solid) to eliminate any competition with the major design element.

- The foreground is the space in which the major design element appears. It should, therefore, carry the dominant color or pattern.

- Additional colors may also be placed here *if* the design can accommodate other colors. Any added color must be of secondary importance to the dominant one.

- The area of *accent* is the smallest area and can contain the brightest color within the total design.

- All of the spaces, if treated as just suggested, will give support to the major design element in the block.

- Use conspicuous or more visible colors (warmer, darker, brighter) to establish an element of interest where one may not exist. Thus you also create emphasis.

- Occasionally the major design element is somewhat difficult to identify, in which case the block may be more effectively used in multiples (repeated blocks) that are joined directly together. Surprising areas of emphasis often evolve! You can plan this with graph paper and colored pencils if you have any questions about a particular design.

- Although the contrast of pattern and solids does provide emphasis, the *scale of the pattern* must be appropriate to the size of the space or patch in which it appears.

- Two or more patterns may be combined effectively *if* the *scale of the patterns* differs and they also share a common color.

- *Pleasing proportions* of color are essential to the creation of beautiful patchwork. You must therefore *avoid equal divisions of color* within the spaces of the total design area.

- Arrange color and pattern so it moves a viewer of your patchwork around and through the block design visually. There are two possibilities for this movement of interest: the "looking at everything and seeing nothing" *or* a movement that reflects a smooth flow of visual interest, thus providing a pleasurable experience for every viewer. This kind of movement is *rhythm*.

- But what about the quality of *unity*? *If* all other qualities are present, then you have no worries about the existence of unity! Let me also add that you will no longer see all of the little parts of your design separately (the triangles, squares, patches of color and pattern). You will, instead, see one whole and one that is truly beautiful.

## The Learning Blocks Introduced

We are, at this point, ready to proceed to the block

designs (six of them) that will serve as learning blocks—a first step in what I hope will be a continuing effort to increase the loveliness of patchwork.

Choices are usually made on the basis of the personal appeal of the design itself, the skills required for construction, and the ability of the doer to attain those skills. This, however, is not a "choosing as usual" kind of choosing (that will come later). This time we are choosing for the purpose of learning to do patchwork by doing patchwork, which means that we will need designs that require a range of all the skills necessary to the construction of any given block design.

With all this in mind, I have taken the liberty of making the learning choices for you. The six selected designs are arranged in an order according to the level of the skills required. Thus, they move you gradually from a level of beginner skills into one of intermediate skills and finally to that of advanced skills. The learning blocks therefore collectively contain all five of the sew-easy patch forms; single blocks have a combination of patch forms, 9 or 16 squares, 9 to 24 patches, and 4 to 8 converging seams.

The learning blocks, listed in order of increasing difficulty, are: Nine Patch, Hourglass, Ohio Star, Susannah, Louisiana, and Card Tricks. They can be found in the color photo section and also in black-and-white in Figure 3 (pages 20–25). Chart 1 gives a block analysis of each, from the simplest to the most complicated. In chapters 4 and 5 we will learn how to make the learning blocks. For now, we will look at two of them from the point of view of color.

## Color and Pattern Selection for Two Learning Blocks

Let's examine the visual examples of design principles for coloring blocks beautiful. The color photographs of the six learning blocks (Nine-Patch, Hourglass, Susannah, Ohio Star, Louisiana, and Card Tricks) are offered in the color photo section as how-to examples of effective use of color and pattern. Next, I have provided a detailed review of color and pattern selection and distribution for two of the learning blocks, Ohio Star and Card Tricks. I also call your attention to six additional reviews in Chapter 6.

## Chart 1.  Block Analysis of the Learning Blocks

**NINE-PATCH**

9  squares
9  patches
1  patch form
0  pieced squares
0  bias seams
4  converging seams
8  thicknesses of fabric

**HOURGLASS**

9  squares
14  patches
3  patch forms
3  pieced squares
2  bias seams
4  converging seams
8  thicknesses of fabric

**SUSANNAH**

16  squares
20  patches
2  patch forms
4  pieced squares
4  bias seams
6  converging seams
12  thicknesses of fabric

**OHIO STAR**

9  squares
21  patches
2  patch forms
4  pieced squares
12  bias seams
6  converging seams
12  thicknesses of fabric

**LOUISIANA**

16  squares
24  patches
2  patch forms
8  pieced squares
8  bias seams
8  converging seams
16  thicknesses of fabric

**CARD TRICKS**

9  squares
24  patches
3  patch forms
9  pieced squares
15  bias seams
6  converging seams
12  thicknesses of fabric

All you need do is look and listen attentively to the reviews; take a long, careful look at the completed designs in color; and enjoy what I predict will be a real fun-time learning experience.

8. *Ohio Star.*

## Ohio Star

### Special Characteristics

The four 4-triangle squares containing the colors that represent the three functional areas necessary in every design (background, foreground, accent) are a special characteristic of the Ohio Star (see color page F).

These areas have certain prescribed functions which do, in turn, guide us in the choosing and using of color and pattern to best accommodate the various functions that actually represent the characteristics or qualities we are seeking to establish in sew-easy patchwork. It is therefore imperative that you familiarize yourself with the "doing tools" that make *this* doing a real fun-time activity. First, a definition of the aesthetic qualities so you know exactly what it is you are trying to do (see "What Is Beautiful?" in Chapter 2); second, the Perceptions Chart (Table 10), which tells you how a color or pattern will look in a design before the fabrics are even purchased or stitched into it; third, the general discussion of the functions of color and pattern; and finally, the swatched paste-up of fabric, which is used to evaluate your use of both ingredients *before* the design is ever constructed (p. 70).

This review of the visual how-to's, as illustrated in the Ohio Star, is designed to serve as a walk-through of my efforts to translate color theory into the practicalities of doing patchwork. My comments are arranged around the individual qualities as just referenced.

Why don't we begin by examining the functions of these areas of design? The *background* is the "nesting" or "resting" place for the design itself. It usually consumes the largest amount of space and is therefore the quietest, least competitive color. With this in mind, I have elected to use a soft, warm tint of beige. The *foreground* area contains the major element of the total design, which in this case is the star itself. It requires the dominant color and pattern—the dark teal paisley print. The *accent* area carries the brightest, most visible color—the warm, red-orange minidot print which serves as a supporting element to the star.

### Contributions to the Qualities of Beautiful

**Balance:** A distribution of color that has to do with the necessity of placement of the heavier, more visible colors and patterns as they relate to the lighter, less visible colors. Remember the seesaw? If one child is too light in weight, we add a second child to create the balance that makes the seesaw work again! In the Ohio Star, the combination of beige and red-orange balances the strong darkness of the foreground star.

**Emphasis:** I have mentioned this quality already. Here we do this with color *and* pattern—the paisley print in the dark, deep teal, the bright red-orange of a square placed diagonally around a straight-set square of paisley in the center of the star, the contrast of the solid noncolor of the beige background, which further emphasizes the importance of the star as *the* interest center.

**Scale/Proportion:** Both qualities relate to size, and again, the elements of variety and contrast (difference and opposition) combine to create both qualities. The scale and density of design differs, the pattern is appropriately used in the small triangles, and the unequal divisions of color and pattern are essential to the establishment of pleasing proportions within the total area of design.

**Rhythm:** We have talked about the visibility of the "framing" square in the red-orange print. It *is* the first color we see, but our vision doesn't just stop there—it moves us out to the star shape which, in contrast against the background of beige around it, moves us through the design, back to the center and out again—a path of pleasurable viewing.

**Unity:** Unity is a oneness of design, a togetherness that is essential to the presence of this particular quality. It exists to the degree that the preceding four qualities exist. They do, so the Ohio Star becomes a truly beautiful block design.

### Personal Comments

*Just* in case you may wonder how a reverse of the foreground and accent colors would look, let me tell you that I wondered that too. I can tell you that the use of the swatched paste-up helped me decide this arrangement is better!

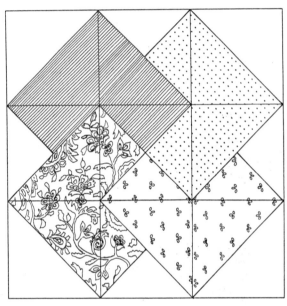

*9. Card Tricks.*

## Card Tricks

### Special Characteristics

Card Tricks has a unique oneness of design despite the distinct differences in all of the elements contained therein: four different colors, four different patterns, three different patch forms (four 2-triangle squares that differ in color and pattern, four 3-triangle squares that differ in color and pattern, and one 4-triangle square that contains four different colors and patterns). See page G of the color section for Card Tricks.

### Contributions to the Qualities of "Beautiful"

The completed design underscores the worth of the Color Perceptions Chart (table 10) as an effective guide for the choosing and using of color and pattern. The chart provides a collection of information that tells us how both ingredients will look in a given block design before the fabrics are purchased or stitched into it. Why don't we measure my use of these elements to create all of the qualities essential to beautiful patchwork?

**Balance:** The *diagonal arrangement* of color—the heavier, more visible shades of dark teal and warm rust as opposed to the lighter, *less* visible shades of aqua and camel—combine to create a pleasing sense of visual balance as the design is viewed right to left or top to bottom.

**Emphasis:** Despite the sameness of shape, the various contrasts of color, pattern, scale and density combine to emphasize the interweaving of chevrons (cards) within this particular block design. Thus, they become an unusual element of the total area, actually the center of attention. Every design must have at least one, sometimes two if the space allows.

**Scale/Proportion:** Even though Card Tricks as shown here carries three different patterns, the contrasting scale and density, plus the fact that they are compatible in color, results in a pleasing sense of both qualities—scale and proportion. The lightness of the background creates an unequal balance of combined color in the dominant element as opposed to that of background. Additionally, our perceptions of the colors as such divides them unequally. This division is essential to the establishment of pleasing proportions.

**Rhythm:** The spectacular use of color and pattern that emphasizes the appearance of interwoven chevrons catches the attention of a viewer, pulling it into and around the entire area of design—a movement of interest that is organized by the contrasts that have also been mentioned. I would therefore say that the quality of rhythm does exist.

**Unity:** By definition, we said that this quality exists to the degree that all others do. Could you disagree with any of my justifications of their presence in the foregoing discussion? If you said "no," let me remind you of the oneness of design that speaks of togetherness of all the differing elements referred to earlier. Thus, the quality of unity is present, for our viewing pleasure.

### Personal Comments

Let me call your attention to two of the usual functions of patterned fabrics illustrated herein, the teal paisley and the camel-colored print. Look at the concealment of seamlines in adjoining triangles in the paisley as contrasted with that of the other three fabrics. Generally speaking, patterns *do* hide construction details, but only if the pattern is densely spaced and includes variations of color.

The camel-colored print is a *directional fabric*, one which offers an interesting point of emphasis within the total design, but only *if* the grainline directions are consistent; they are in our model (see the color photo). Imagine how distracting it would be if the pattern on the four camel-colored triangles forming the chevron ran in different directions!

## Making a Swatched Paste-up and Shopping for Fabric

Now it's time to go shopping! Translate your shopping colors into actual fabrics for your learning blocks:

- Browse in the section of the store that has fabrics appropriate for patchwork. We have already determined that the fabric of choice is 100% cotton!

- Combine bolts of fabric that represent the color families of the individual harmonies you have elected to use. Stand back and look at your selections with a critical eye. Ask yourself some questions—questions that have to do with the how-to's just reviewed. Make any changes you wish. This kind of trial-and-error choosing doesn't involve money. You are looking at and thinking about which is actually fun to do! You are *learning to choose by choosing*, remember?

- Once you are satisfied with these tentative choices, purchase a 2″ strip of each fabric. Keep them in separate combinations as named on the index cards you made earlier. Clip them to the proper card to avoid any confusion later.

Next, evaluate your choices *before* you purchase the fabrics for your learning blocks:

- Make a swatched paste-up of the learning block you are ready to construct. This mock-up serves as a trial block, except that it is done with a scaled drawing, swatches of fabric and paste. Blank copies of the forms you will need (the 9-Square Grid and the 16-Square Choose a Design) appear in the Appendix. Look back at the learning blocks illustrated in Figure 3 if you need any help with this scaled drawing. Choose the correct grid on which to work and trace or copy it onto a paper.

- Cut the strips of selected fabric into squares and then into triangles as needed, and play with them within the spaces of the design, like fitting pieces of a jigsaw puzzle together! Shuffle the fabric shapes around until you are satisfied with the look of the total design.

- Before you secure the fabric swatches in the chosen spaces, go back and review briefly both the *verbal* and *visual* suggestions for effective distribution of color and pattern.

- When you are confident that the mock-up exhibits the characteristics or qualities of beautiful, secure the patches in their spaces. Then *go back to the store* and purchase the yardage, plus other supplies, as suggested on the Supplies List.

## Preparation of Fabric

Next, prepare your fabrics for a doing that is perfectly beautiful and sew easy.

- Using warm water and a mild detergent, wash and dry your fabrics on gentle cycles until they are damp dry. Be sure to check that they are colorfast.

- Establish the straight horizontal grain by tearing in a crosswise direction at both the upper and lower edges of each piece of fabric to remove any edges that aren't straight. Clip through the selvage and into the fabric to begin the tearing.

- Fold the fabric in half vertically, with both selvages aligned perfectly. If the horizontal edges are not also aligned, the fabric is off-grain and must be straightened before it is used (see Fig. 13, pg. 93).

- Remember, too, that the crosswise thread *runs continuously* across the fabric, so clip off a *small* triangle at each corner of the selvage to avoid any ravelling of this crosswise thread.

- Press across the torn edges, stretching them gently ahead of the iron to remove the rippling effect caused by the tearing.

- Straighten the fabric as suggested (in Figure 13), and continue with your pressing until the entire length is nice and smooth. Something else to remember—*pressing is not ironing!* Do not move the iron back and forth, just straight down, or you risk stretching the fabric.

- Continue to check for the straight-of-grain and

adjust as necessary. Much can be accomplished with the iron if you are careful to pull gently against the off-grain direction as you press the fabric.

- Trim off the selvages and discard them. They are too tightly woven for quilting.

## Supplies List

### Fabric
- ¼ yard of each color and/or print appearing in a given block design. (I suggest muslin as a background and prints and/or solids in harmonizing colors for the other areas)
- 100% cotton is preferred: It is soft, easy to work with, and available in traditional colors and/or patterns
- Coordinated colors/patterns and variations in value—light, medium, dark—provide added interest and design impact.

### Needles
- Sharps, in assorted sizes
- Quilting betweens, sizes 3 through 9. Shorter needles *help* you make shorter, uniform stitches in quilting.

### Pins
- Straight ballpoint dressmaker pins
- T pins or long bead-top ones for pin-basting prior to quilting.

### Thread
- Quilting cotton *or*
- Cotton-covered polyester in a neutral color, size 50

### Thimble
- One that fits—thimbles save your fingers! Leather ones are available in some areas; they may be easier for beginners.

### Scissors
- Straight cutting ones that are very sharp!
- A trimming-size scissors also is helpful; I could say they are almost a must.

### Plastic see-through quilter's ruler
- 12″ long is enough

### Marking pens or pencils
- A #2 soft lead pencil that is very sharp!
- A fine-point accounting pen works well. Avoid

pens or pencils that smudge or run in water. Thick, stubby marking points are inaccurate and to be avoided.

## Batting

- 1½ yards of traditional-weight bonded polyester batting, which provides uniformity of thicknesses, greater loft than cotton, and ease in quilting. Also it is washable and light in weight.
- Ask for batting that is made specifically for quilting.

## Backing or lining

- 1¼ yards of muslin will do for all six learning blocks. (100% permanent-press cotton is desirable; it may be more costly, but looks great!)

## Pencil sharpener

- For keeping pencil points thin and sharp. Markings are more accurate when pencils are sharp.

## Graph paper, colored pencils

- Useful in duplication of designs, to see how they will look in multiples.

## Paste or glue

- Necessary for making swatched paste-up trial block (one that is pasted together rather than stitched together).
- Iron and tabletop ironing board. The board is portable, therefore easy to use. The size of board is also a plus for pressing seams, small patches, etc.

The following aids are also necessary if you plan to use the completed designs as pillows.

## Fabric

- An additional ½ yard (18″) of one of the fabrics for corded edging and a pillow back. (The other ¼ yard length will provide the borders of the pillow top.) (Chapter 5 gives more information on pillows.)

## Cord

- 2 yards #60 cord for edge finish. Other edges may be used: ruffles, lace, embroidered trims, etc.

## Coil zipper

- The zipper's length should be 2″ shorter than the finished width of the block, including its borders. Other fasteners for pillow covers are possible: snaps, gripper tape, Velcro, or even thread.

## Pillow Form

- Could be store-purchased or homemade.
- A 12″ finished quilt block with a 2″ border will require a 16″ × 16″ pillow form. This is a standard size.

# Planning an Heirloom on Paper

## Introduction

Interdependence, in retrospect. We learned in the very beginning of this text that sew-easy is more than just the doing of patchwork—that the entire process involves thinking, looking, learning, planning, and *then* doing! Though I have called these *preliminaries*, each topic is essential to the creation of patchwork that is beautiful. And that also means a creation that is fun, and of course, so easy! Since each topic builds on those that precede, and planning is the last one of the four, I think it might be helpful at this point to go back and tie them all together with a few brief comments.

When we think about the evolution of patchwork from a functional necessity to a beautiful art form, we realize that this lovely needle skill was (and is) perpetuated through a cycle of viewing and doing beautiful patchwork. It will continue as such so long as the cycle continues. And this is the primary purpose of the thinking chapter (Chapter 1)—moving *you* into a doing that *is* truly beautiful!

When we look at the contrasts between the tangibles of patchworking, we discover the characteristics that make it beautiful—truly a joy forever! And this is the established goal for sew-easy.

As we learn how to achieve the ultimate accomplishment of these characteristics through positive choices (block design, fabric, color and pattern, even tools to work with), we are able to identify the skills necessary to do so, thereby protecting the legacy of patchwork for generations yet to come. That, if Mr. Keats' words in verse are true, is how we increase the loveliness of an already beautiful piece of patchwork.

This brings us to the topic of planning, which is fundamental to the successful performance of these identified skills. As an experienced patchworker, *I* see planning as an imaginary doing that seeks to eliminate all of the barriers to beautiful *before* we actually *sew* anything! It is our assurance that the patchwork we create does become a part of a continuing cycle of viewing and doing, that it will never pass into nothingness simply because it *is* beautiful!

In order for us to better understand the process of planning as it relates to patchwork, there are three questions that will be helpful to you in this regard: What is planning? Why is planning important? How is planning accomplished? Let's talk about them in this same order. My dictionary tells me that planning is the listing of sequential steps that move one toward the accomplishment of a predetermined goal.

We can put it in simple terms and say that a plan for patchwork is a list—in consecutive order—of all the things one must do to create the "joys forever" kind of patchwork as discussed in Chapter 2.

The importance of "why" is more easily understood if we think of planning as a show and tell. It shows us where we are going—the goal we wish to accomplish. It tells us how to get there—like a roadmap for travelling. It shows us how to deal with any emergency as we go—how to avoid the detours to beautiful work. It tells us when we have arrived—when beautiful is achieved. Surely all of this makes planning a requisite of successful patchworking.

Now, the last question: How is planning accomplished? Two ways, and I suspect you are familiar with both—either with a think-about plan or a paper plan. A think-about plan is just what it says, a plan that you think about but store inside your head. A paper plan is one that you also think about but then write down on paper.

While a think-about plan is better than nothing, it doesn't work very well for a detailed procedure like patchworking, for obvious reasons. Most of us have a tendency to forget some of what we think about, to change our minds on impulse, to ignore or overlook details that might be critical to the successful outcome of an activity. Also important is the fact that think-about plans are difficult to convey to someone else. As a result, they have a tendency to become "my" plans, and "my" plans limit sharing with others as a test for effectiveness. Just think of all the joys of sharing that are lost—both to you and others.

I will readily agree that planning on paper takes a lot of time for careful study, perceptive thinking, and thoroughness of preparation. But—it works. Why? Because we can look at a written plan any time we choose, we can study it critically, we can walk through it in our imagination. We can share the walk-through with others as a means of evaluation. Then when all of this is done, we can change the plan, adjust or rearrange the plan, even rewrite it if necessary. We can move through the plan over and over in our minds until we feel the envisioned end result (the predetermined goal) can be attained with ease. A paper plan that is carefully formulated can change frustration into fun, ordinary into beautiful. Moreover, the time spent in *planning* patchwork is regained ten times over in its *doing*—and with immeasurable pleasure for doers and viewers alike.

Since you are learning how to create beautiful, this seems just the right time for us to walk through two paper plans. I'm glad they *can* be shared! The first is a general plan, the second is a specific plan. Both will be helpful to you as a successful doer of patchwork.

## A General Plan from Start to Finish

This plan serves as an outline or overview of the entire process of patchworking. It is presented in a sequence of steps that illustrate the interdependence of the preliminaries to doing: thinking, looking, learning, planning. It is designed to move you from a simple interest in patchwork into its doing and all the way through to a finished and beautiful work. It can serve as a kind of checklist or base that you may run back and touch to make sure *no* detail that might affect the final appearance of your patchwork has been overlooked. You can refer to the earlier pages of this book for further clarification as you work through the plan. The parts that haven't been discussed yet will be explained in detail in Chapter 5. Here it is:

**1.** Choose a block design.

**2.** Color it beautiful (in your imagination—at this point you are just *thinking* about color choices)

**3.** Learn how to see (all the things you need to know about getting there)

**4.** Review your think-about decision concerning color

**5.** Add some think-abouts for color distribution (where you'll put them within the block designs)

**6.** Go shopping
  • Play with fabric combinations
  • Make a tentative choice of fabric colors/patterns
  • Purchase 2″ or 3″ of each fabric (you can still change your mind at this point)

**7.** Evaluate your choices against a standard for good design
  • Make a swatched paste-up of your chosen block design
  • Check the paste-up against the established standards of good design for large areas of patchwork as related to *visual* and *emo-*

*tional* pleasure (the recipe for good design in Chapter 2)
- Adjust your choice if necessary

**8.** Purchase all the things you need, including the fabric, *but* only enough for a trial block. (You are still learning, remember?) We hope you'll buy yards very soon.

**9.** Prepare your fabric for doing
- Establish grainlines (horizontally tear off the unsquare ends; vertically trim the selvages)
- Wash the fabric (use detergent with warm water)
- Press and straighten the grainline; stretch ahead of the iron to remove the rippling effect of tearing. Check the grainline and adjust the fabric further if necessary

**10.** Put all of your plans on paper. We will discuss how in the next part of this chapter, using the following charts:
- Choose a Design
- Look and See
- List All the Givens
- Color Blocks Beautiful
- Square Things Away
- Tie It All Together

At last! You're ready now for the *doing* aspect of planning!

**11.** Measure and cut squares. For trial blocks, cut them singly. This will be discussed in detail in Chapter 5)

**12.** Mark the sewing and cutting lines on the squares
- For *all* squares: mark ¼″ seam allowance around the 4 outside edges
- For *pieced squares:* mark cutting lines and ¼″ seam allowances on either side of these. (This will be explained in Chapter 5)

**13.** Construct the pieced squares (this will be explained in detail in Chapter 5)
- Stitch the designated squares together
- Cut the units apart
- Finger-press the seams directionally to reduce their bulk
- Stitch 2 units together to form a square
- Finger-press the seams on the pieced unit

**14.** Lay out the squares for assembly (see Chapter 5)
- Place them right-side up
- Examine the directional turn of crossed seam allowances
- Adjust as necessary
- Re-press the squares carefully (remember that pressing is *not* ironing)

**15.** Assemble the squares (see Chapter 5).

# A Specific Plan

The specific plan is actually a written record of the think-about decisions outlined in the first nine steps of the general plan. It serves as a transition from planning into doing and is vital to both.

The "easy, fun, and beautiful" promised at the outset of *Perfect Patchwork* is dependent on the accuracy of the information you put in this record form. Because you must rely on words you can see rather than those you can hear, it is essential that you "listen" carefully to the instructions as offered. They may, at first reading, seem too detailed, but you are *learning*, remember? Once you do that, you are free to simplify the process as you see fit and without jeopardizing the desired outcome of your patching efforts. In the meantime, just listen, do as I say, and watch every single patch fall into place! Easy as pie!

Why don't we walk through the format of the planning forms first, and then look at the way they are used? The forms are a series of completion charts, each of which builds on those that precede it. Let's see what they look like.

# Choose a Design: Reduced Block Outlines

The first charts, Choose a Design, have a reduced block form within which the design to be planned is drawn. Swatches of your chosen fabrics are then pasted or colored in so that you know in advance *where* it is you are going and, additionally, *when* you have arrived. Depending on the design you will need either the 9-square or 16-square version.

## Choose a Design: 9 Squares

This illustration serves as a kind of road map. It shows you *where* you are going. It tells you *when* you get there. Duplicate the design you wish to construct within the reduced block form. Color or paste in swatches of the fabrics you have selected.

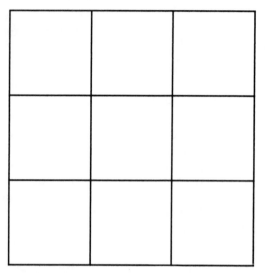

**Name of block design:** _____

## Choose a Design: 16 Squares

This illustration serves as a kind of road map—it shows you *where* you are going. It tells you *when* you get there. Duplicate the design you wish to construct within the reduced block form. Color or paste in swatches of the fabrics you have selected.

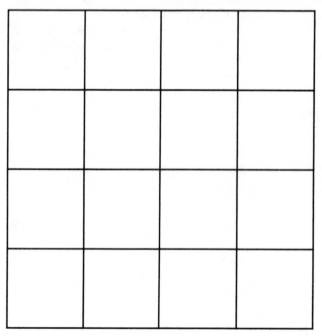

**Name of block design:** _____

# Look and See
# (Form and Color)

The second charts, Look and See, are designed to help you see all the things you *need* to see. You duplicate the block design you have chosen, but in separated squares. You identify squares and fabrics for easier reference in planning and doing. Depending on your design, you will need either the 9-square or 16-square version.

---

## Look and See (Form and Color): 9 Squares

**Name of block design:** _____

When you can visualize a total block design in squares and patches, the entire process of patchworking—planning, cutting, piecing, assembly—becomes sew easy it's fun to do. But planning comes first and in the order listed below:

- Draw in the design you wish to construct.
- Color or paste in swatches of your chosen fabrics.
- Number the squares 1 to 9 from left to right and top to bottom.
- Letter the fabrics A, B, C, D, etc.

# Look and See (Form and Color): 16 Squares

**Name of block design:** _____

When you can visualize a total block design in squares and patches, the entire process of patchworking—planning, cutting, piecing, assembly—becomes sew easy it's fun to do. But planning comes first, in the order listed below:

- Draw in the design you wish to construct.
- Color or paste in swatches of your chosen fabrics.
- Number the squares 1 to 16 from left to right and top to bottom.
- Letter the fabrics A, B, C, D, etc.

# List All the Givens (Basic Information)

The third chart, List All the Givens, is a "fill-in-the-blanks" collection of basic information, which serves as a reference for further planning. The emphasis here is on the design factors that affect the ease with which we can create the visible characteristics of beautiful patchwork (see Chapter 3 for further information).

# List All the Givens (Basic Information)

**Name of block design:** _____

Study the design presented in "Choose a Design" and complete the following blanks:

Finished size of block design[a] _____

Total number of squares in block[b] _____

Finished size of each square _____

Total number of patches in block[c] _____

Number of different fabrics needed _____

See the square forms illustrated below. Write in the total number needed of each in the space provided.

Total number of square forms[b] _____

| **1-patch** | **2-triangle** | **4-triangle** | **3-triangle** | **4-square** |
|---|---|---|---|---|
| No. _____ | No. _____ | No. _____ | No. _____ | No. _____ |

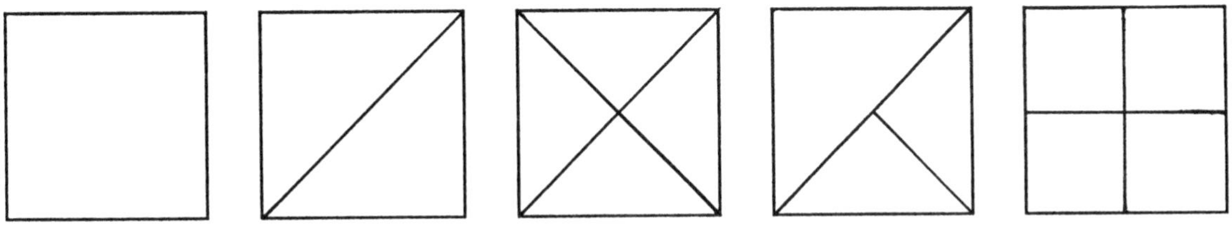

_____

[a] Finished size of all blocks in our book is 12″ × 12″.

[b] Total number of squares and total number of square forms must be the same.

[c] See the block designs in Figure 3 for this information (Chapter 3).

## Color Blocks Beautiful

The fourth chart, Color Blocks Beautiful, relates to the use of color in squares and patches as a means of creating designs that are truly beautiful. This information will be of particular value to you in piecing and assembly. The colors are from the Look and See Chart.

## Color Blocks Beautiful

Name of block design: _____

| Swatched square form[a] | How many in block design? | Placement in block design (square numbers) |
|---|---|---|
| (empty square) | _____ | _____ |
| (empty square) | _____ | _____ |
| (empty square) | _____ | _____ |
| (empty square) | _____ | _____ |

[a] Duplicate each square in the block design that *differs* from the others in form and/or color. (Use additional pages as necessary.)

## Square Things Away

The fifth chart, Square Things Away, helps you determine the exact number, size, and color of whole-cloth squares you need to cut for sew-easy construction of your chosen block design. Though all five of the patch forms are included here for your review, only those that apply to a given design should appear in your planning form for that particular design. You can get the information you need from the Look and See chart.

# Square Things Away

**Name of block design:** _____

Look carefully at the block design illustrated in Look and See. The chart below indicates what you are to look for. Write down what you see in the spaces that are provided. Read each column heading carefully and double-check your counting.

| Square form | Number of whole-cloth squares in block design, by fabric | Number of squares to cut, by fabric | Cutting size, of squares, by fabric[a] |
|---|---|---|---|
| **Whole-cloth** | **Fabric A** _____ | _____ | _____ |
| | **Fabric B** _____ | _____ | _____ |
| | **Fabric C** _____ | _____ | _____ |
| | **Fabric D** _____ | _____ | _____ |
| **Number in block design** _____ | **Fabric E** _____ | _____ | _____ |

[a] Cutting size = finished size + ½″ for whole-cloth squares.

| Square form | Number of triangles from 2-triangle squares, by fabric[b] | Number of squares to cut, by fabric[b] | Cutting size of squares, by fabric[c] |
|---|---|---|---|
| **2-triangle** | **Fabric A** _____ | _____ | _____ |
| | **Fabric B** _____ | _____ | _____ |
| | **Fabric C** _____ | _____ | _____ |
| | **Fabric D** _____ | _____ | _____ |
| **Number in block design** _____ | **Fabric E** _____ | _____ | _____ |

[b] Number of triangles divided by 2 = number of squares to cut. A full square is required for any number of triangles less than 2.
[c] Cutting size = finished size of pieced square + ⅞″ for 2-triangle squares.

## Square Things Away, continued

| Square form | Number of triangles from 4-triangle squares, by fabric | Number of squares to cut, by fabric[d] | Cutting size of squares, by fabric[e] |
|---|---|---|---|
| **4-triangle** | Fabric A _____ | _____ | _____ |
| | Fabric B _____ | _____ | _____ |
| | Fabric C _____ | _____ | _____ |
| | Fabric D _____ | _____ | _____ |
| **Number in block design** _____ | Fabric E _____ | _____ | _____ |

[d] Number of triangles divided by 4 = number of squares to cut. A full square is required for any number of triangles less than 4.
[e] Cutting size = finished size of pieced square + 1⅜".

| Square form | Number of triangles in 1-triangle half of squares, by fabric | Number of squares to cut, by fabric[f] | Cutting size of squares, by fabric[g] |
|---|---|---|---|
| **3-triangle** | Fabric A _____ | _____ | _____ |
| | Fabric B _____ | _____ | _____ |
| | Fabric C _____ | _____ | _____ |
| | Fabric D _____ | _____ | _____ |
| **Number in block design** _____ | Fabric E _____ | _____ | _____ |

[f] Number of triangles divided by 2 = the number of squares to cut for the 1-triangle half. A full square is required for any number of triangles less than 2.
[g] Cutting size = finished size + ⅞".

*Note:* When we look carefully at the 3-triangle square form, what we actually see is half of a 2-triangle square form and half of a 4-triangle square form. This will require the provision of information for *both* square forms. Read each column heading carefully and double-check your *counting*.

**Square Things Away, continued**

| Square form | Number of triangles in 2-triangle half of squares, by fabric | Number of squares to cut, by fabric[h] | Cutting size of squares, by fabric[i] |
|---|---|---|---|
| 3-triangle | Fabric A _____ | _____ | _____ |
| | Fabric B _____ | _____ | _____ |
| | Fabric C _____ | _____ | _____ |
| | Fabric D _____ | _____ | _____ |
| Number in block design _____ | Fabric E _____ | _____ | _____ |

[h] Number of triangles divided by 4 = number of squares to cut for the two-triangle half. A full square is required for any number of triangles less than 4.

[i] Cutting size = finished size + $1\frac{3}{8}''$.

| Square form | Number of small squares within the larger square, by fabric | Number of rectangles to cut, by fabric | Cutting size of rectangles, by fabric[j] |
|---|---|---|---|
| 4-square | Fabric A _____ | _____ | _____ |
| | Fabric B _____ | _____ | _____ |
| | Fabric C _____ | _____ | _____ |
| | Fabric D _____ | _____ | _____ |
| Number in block design _____ | Fabric E _____ | _____ | _____ |

[j] Cut two small squares together as a rectangle. See text page 97 for details.

# Tie It All Together: A Summary Chart for Cutting

The sixth chart, Tie It All Together, is a summary of information required for cutting the whole-cloth squares needed for constructing the pieced squares in any block design. This form moves you out of planning and into doing without interruption. After all, planning is a continual process.

# Tie It All Together: A Summary Chart for Cutting

Name of block design: _____

| Which fabrics? | Fabric swatch[a] | How many squares? | How big? | Patch form involved? |
|---|---|---|---|---|
| A | | ___ ___ ___ | ___ ___ ___ | ___ ___ ___ |
| B | | ___ ___ ___ | ___ ___ ___ | ___ ___ ___ |
| C | | ___ ___ ___ | ___ ___ ___ | ___ ___ ___ |
| D | | ___ ___ ___ | ___ ___ ___ | ___ ___ ___ |
| E | | ___ ___ ___ | ___ ___ ___ | ___ ___ ___ |

[a] Color or paste in the fabric swatches identified in Look and See.

## Completed Charts for the Six Learning Blocks

Now that you have been introduced to the six planning charts (Choose a Design, Look and See, List All the Givens, Color Blocks Beautiful, Square Things Away, and Tie It All Together), it's time to show you exactly how they work. I have done this by filling out the charts for my own versions of the six learning blocks: Nine-Patch, Hourglass, Susannah, Ohio Star, Louisiana, and Card Tricks. The fabric patterns you will find in these charts correspond to the patterns in the fabrics I chose—see the color photo section for comparison. You will need to refer to these completed planning charts when you create your *own* versions of the learning blocks, later on.

# Completed Planning Charts for
# the Nine-Patch Design

The completed Nine-Patch charts are based on my
model, shown in the color section (color page C).

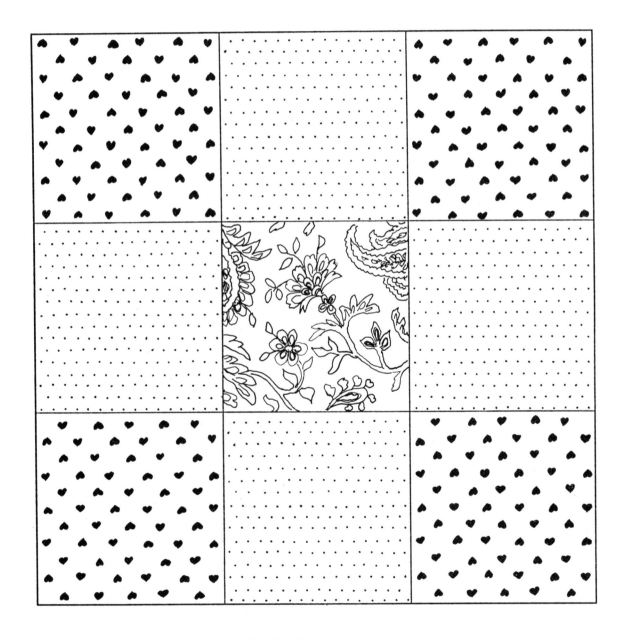

## Choose a Design: 9 Squares

This illustration serves as a kind of road map: it shows you *where* you are going. It tells you *when* you get there.
Duplicate the design you wish to construct within the reduced block form. Color or paste in swatches of the fabrics
you have selected.

**Name of block design:** *Nine Patch*

# Look and See (Form and Color): 9 Squares

**Name of block design:** _Nine-Patch_

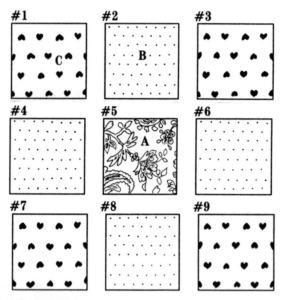

- Draw in the design you wish to construct.
- Color or paste in swatches of your chosen fabrics.
- Number the squares 1 to 9 from left to right and top to bottom.
- Letter the fabrics A, B, C, D, etc.

# List All the Givens (Basic Information)

**Name of block design:** _Nine-Patch_

Study the design presented in Choose a Design and complete the following blanks:

Finished size of block design _12″ × 12″_

Total number of squares in block[a] ___9___

Finished size of each square _4″ × 4″_

Total number of patches in block ___9___

Number of different fabrics needed ___3___

See square forms illustrated below. Write in the total number needed of each in the space provided.

Total number of square forms[a] ___9___

| whole-cloth | 2-triangle | 4-triangle | 3-triangle | 4-square |
|---|---|---|---|---|
| No. _9_ | No. _0_ | No. _0_ | No. _0_ | No. _0_ |

[a] Total number of squares and total number of square forms must be the same.

# Color Blocks Beautiful

**Name of block design:** _Nine-Patch_

| Swatched square form[a] | How many in block design? | Placement in block design (square numbers) |
|---|---|---|
| | _1_ | _#5_ |
| | _4_ | _#2, 4, 6, 8_ |
| | _4_ | _#1, 3, 7, 9_ |

[a] Duplicate each square in the block design that _differs_ from the others in form and/or color. (Use additional pages as necessary.)

# Square Things Away

**Name of block design:** _Nine-Patch_

Look carefully at the block design illustrated in Look and See. The chart below indicates what you are to look for. Write down what you see in the spaces that are provided. Read each column heading carefully and double-check your counting.

| Square form | Number of whole-cloth squares in block design, by fabric | Number of squares to cut, by fabric | Cutting size, of squares, by fabric |
|---|---|---|---|
| **Whole-cloth** | Fabric A _1_ | _1_ | _4½" × 4½"_ |
| | Fabric B _4_ | _4_ | _4½" × 4½"_ |
| | Fabric C _4_ | _4_ | _4½" × 4½"_ |

**Number in block design** _9_

# Tie It All Together: A Summary Chart for Cutting

**Name of block design:** _Nine-Patch_

| Which fabrics? | Fabric swatch[a] | How many squares? | How big? | Patch form involved? |
|---|---|---|---|---|
| A | | _1_ | $4^{1}/_{2}'' \times 4^{1}/_{2}''$ | _Whole-Cloth_ |
| B | | _4_ | $4^{1}/_{2}'' \times 4^{1}/_{2}''$ | _Whole-Cloth_ |
| C | | _4_ | $4^{1}/_{2}'' \times 4^{1}/_{2}''$ | _Whole-Cloth_ |

[a] Color or paste in the fabric swatches identified in Look and See.

## Completed Planning Charts for Hourglass

The completed Hourglass charts are based on my model, shown in the color section (color page B).

### Choose a Design: 9 Squares

This illustration serves as a kind of road map: it shows you *where* you are going. It tells you *when* you get there. Duplicate the design you wish to construct within the reduced block form. Color or paste in swatches of the fabrics you have selected.

**Name of block design:** *Hourglass*

# Look and See (Form and Color): 9 Squares

Name of block design: *Hourglass*

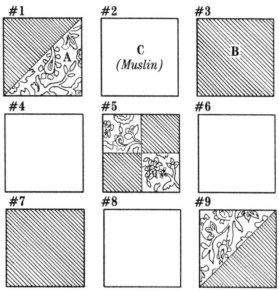

- Draw in the design you wish to construct.
- Color or paste in swatches of your chosen fabrics.
- Number squares 1 to 9 from left to right and top to bottom.
- Letter the fabrics A, B, C, D, etc.

# List All the Givens (Basic Information)

Name of block design: *Hourglass*

Study the design presented in Choose a Design and complete the following blanks:

Finished size of block design *12″ × 12″*

Total number of squares in block[a] *9*

Finished size of each square *4½″*

Total number of patches in block *14*

Number of different fabrics needed *3*

See the square forms illustrated below. Write in the total number needed of each in the space provided.

Total number of square forms[a] *9*

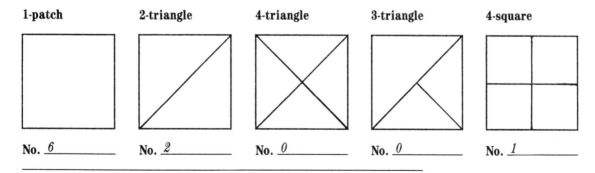

| 1-patch | 2-triangle | 4-triangle | 3-triangle | 4-square |
|---------|------------|------------|------------|----------|
| No. *6* | No. *2* | No. *0* | No. *0* | No. *1* |

[a] Total number of squares and total number of square forms must be the same.

# Color Blocks Beautiful

**Name of block design:** _Hourglass_

| Swatched square form[a] | How many in block design? | Placement in block design (square numbers) |
|---|---|---|
| | _1_ | _#5_ |
| | _2_ | _#1, 9_ |
| | _2_ | _#3, 7_ |
| (Muslin) | _4_ | _#2, 4, 6, 8_ |

[a] Duplicate each square in the block design that _differs_ from the others in form and/or color. (Use additional pages as necessary.)

# Square Things Away

**Name of block design:** _Hourglass_

Look carefully at the block design illustrated in Look and See. The chart below indicates what you are to look for. Write down what you see in the spaces that are provided. Read each column heading carefully and double-check your counting.

| Square form | Number of whole-cloth squares in block design, by fabric | Number of squares to cut, by fabric | Cutting size, of squares, by fabric |
|---|---|---|---|
| **Whole-cloth** | Fabric A _____ | _____ | _____ |
| | Fabric B _2_ | _2_ | _$4\frac{1}{2}'' \times 4\frac{1}{2}''$_ |
| | Fabric C _4_ (Muslin) | _4_ | _$4\frac{1}{2}'' \times 4\frac{1}{2}''$_ |
| **Number in block design** _6_ | | | |

| Square form | Number of triangles in 2-triangle squares, by fabric | Number of squares to cut, by fabric[a] | Cutting size of squares, by fabric |
|---|---|---|---|
| **2-triangle** | Fabric A _2_ | _1_ | _$4\frac{7}{8}'' \times 4\frac{7}{8}''$_ |
| 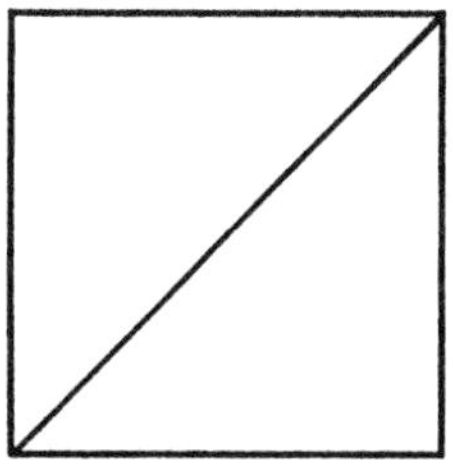 | Fabric B _2_ | _1_ | _$4\frac{7}{8}'' \times 4\frac{7}{8}''$_ |
| **Number in block design** _2_ | | | |

[a] Number of triangles divided by 2 = number of squares to cut. A full square is required for any number of triangles less than 2.

## Square Things Away, Hourglass, continued

| Square form | Number of small squares within the larger square, by fabric | Number of rectangles to cut, by fabric | Rectangle cutting size, by fabric[b] |
|---|---|---|---|
| 4-square | Fabric A _2_ | _2_ | 2½″ × 5″ |
| | Fabric B _2_ | _2_ | 2½″ × 5″ |

Number in block design __1__

[b] Cut rectangles, out of which the smaller squares will be made. This makes the piecing sew easy. See text in Chapter 5 for piecing details.

# Tie It All Together: A Summary Chart for Cutting

Name of block design: ___Hourglass___

| Which fabrics? | Fabric swatch[a] | How many squares? | How big? | Patch form involved? |
|---|---|---|---|---|
| A | | _1_ | 4⅞″ × 4⅞″ | 2-Triangle |
| | | _1_ | 2½″ × 5″ | 4-Square |
| | | | | |
| B | | _1_ | 4⅞″ × 4⅞″ | 2-Triangle |
| | | _2_ | 4½″ × 4½″ | 1-Patch |
| | | _1_ | 2½″ × 5″ | 4-Square |
| C (Muslin) | | _4_ | 4½″ | 1-Patch |
| | | | | |
| | | | | |

[a] Color or paste in the fabric swatches identified in Look and See.

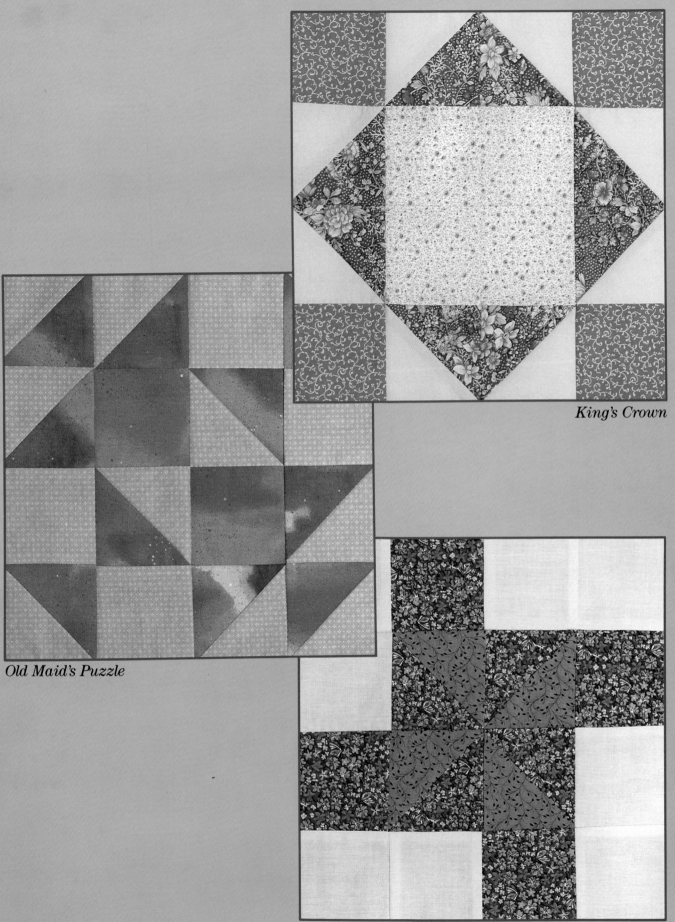

Windmill

King's Crown

Old Maid's Puzzle

A

*Susannah*

*Hourglass*

*Jacob's Ladder*

**B**

Road to Oklahoma

Shoofly

Nine-Patch

C

*Triplet*

*Attic Windows*

*Ship*

Dutchman's Puzzle

Crosses and Losses

Helen's Choice

E

Battlegrounds

Clown's Choice

Ohio Star

F

Card Tricks

Clay's Choice

Double 4-Patch

*Puss in the Corner*

*Evening Star*

*Louisiana*

**H**

## Completed Planning Charts for Susannah

The completed Susannah charts are based on my model, shown in the color section (color page B).

### Choose a Design: 16 Squares

This illustration serves as a kind of road map. It shows you *where* you are going. It tells you *when* you get there. Duplicate the design you wish to construct within the reduced block form. Color or place in swatches of the fabrics you have selected.

Name of block design: *Susannah*

# Look and See (Form and Color): 16 Squares

**Name of block design:** _Susannah_

When you can visualize a total block design in squares and patches, the entire process of patchworking—planning, cutting, piecing, assembly—becomes sew easy it's fun to do. But planning comes first and in the order listed below:

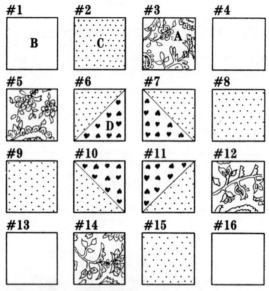

- Draw in the design you wish to construct.
- Color or paste in swatches of your chosen fabrics.
- Number the squares 1 to 16 from left to right and top to bottom.
- Letter the fabrics A, B, C, D, etc.

# List All the Givens (Basic Information)

**Name of block design:** _Susannah_

Study the design presented in Choose a Design and complete the following blanks:

Finished size of block design _12" × 12"_

Total number of squares in block[a] _16_

Finished size of each square _3" × 3"_

Total number of patches in block _20_

Number of different fabrics needed _4_

See square forms illustrated below. Write in the total number needed of each in the space provided.

Total number of square forms _16_

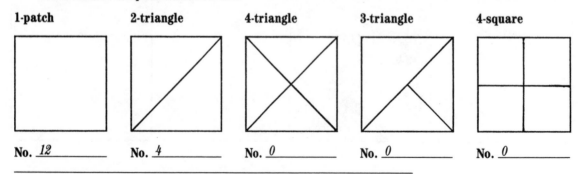

| 1-patch | 2-triangle | 4-triangle | 3-triangle | 4-square |
|---------|-----------|-----------|-----------|----------|
| No. _12_ | No. _4_ | No. _0_ | No. _0_ | No. _0_ |

[a] Total number of squares and total number of square forms must be the same.

66

# Color Blocks Beautiful

Name of block design: _Susannah_

| Swatched square form[a] | How many in block design? | Placement in block design (square numbers) |
|---|---|---|
| | 4 | #3, 5, 12, 15 |
| | 4 | #2, 8, 9, 14 |
| | 4 | #6, 7, 10, 11 |
| *(Muslin)* | 4 | #1, 4, 13, 16 |

[a] Duplicate each square in the block design that *differs* from the others in form and/or color. (Use additional pages as necessary.)

# Square Things Away

**Name of block design:** _Susannah_

Look carefully at the block design illustrated in Look and See. The chart below indicates what you are to look for. Write down what you see in the spaces that are provided. Read each column heading carefully and double-check your counting.

| Square form | Number of whole-cloth squares in block design, by fabric | Number of squares to cut, by fabric | Cutting size, of squares, by fabric |
|---|---|---|---|
| **Whole-cloth** | Fabric A __4__ | 4 | 3½″ × 3½″ |
| | Fabric B __4__ (Muslin) | 4 | 3½″ × 3½″ |
| | Fabric C __4__ | 4 | 3½″ × 3½″ |
| | Fabric D __0__ | 0 | 0 |
| **Number in block design __12__** | | | |

| Square form | Number of triangles from 2-triangle squares, by fabric[a] | Number of squares to cut, by fabric | Cutting size of squares, by fabric |
|---|---|---|---|
| **2-triangle** | Fabric A __0__ | | |
| 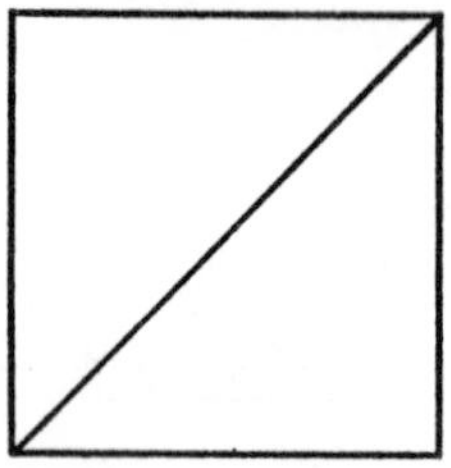 | Fabric B __0__ | | |
| | Fabric C __2__ | 2 | 3⅞″ × 3⅞″ |
| | Fabric D __2__ | 2 | 3⅞″ × 3⅞″ |
| **Number in block design __4__** | | | |

[a] Number of triangles divided by 2 = number of squares to cut. A full square is required for any number of triangles fewer than 2.

# Tie It All Together: A Summary Chart for Cutting

Name of block design: *Susannah*

| Which fabrics? | Fabric swatch[a] | How many squares? | How big? | Patch form involved? |
|---|---|---|---|---|
| A | | 4 | 3½" × 3½" | 1-Patch |
| B (Muslin) | | 4 | 3½" × 3½" | 1-Patch |
| C | | 4 | 3½" × 3½" | 1-Patch |
| | | 2 | 3⅞" × 3⅞" | 2-Triangle |
| D | | 2 | 3⅞" × 3⅞" | 2-Triangle |

[a] Color or paste in the fabric swatches identified in Look and See.

## Completed Planning Charts for the Ohio Star

The completed Ohio Star charts are based on my model, shown in the color section (color page F).

### Choose a Design: 9 Squares

This illustration serves as a kind of road map. It shows you *where* you are going. It tells you *when* you get there. Duplicate the design you wish to construct within the reduced block form. Color or paste in swatches of the fabrics you have selected.

**Name of block design:**  *Ohio Star*

# Look and See (Form and Color): 9 Squares

**Name of block design:** _Ohio Star_

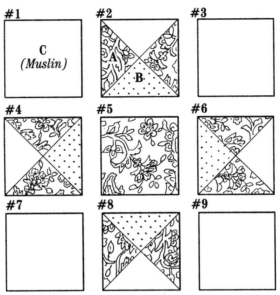

- Draw in the design you wish to construct.
- Color or paste in swatches of your chosen fabrics.
- Number the squares 1 to 9 from left to right and top to bottom.
- Letter the fabrics A, B, C, D, etc.

# List All the Givens (Basic Information)

**Name of block design:** _Ohio Star_

Study the design presented in Choose a Design and complete the following blanks:

Finished size of block design[a] _12″ × 12″_

Total number of squares in block[b] _9_

Finished size of each square _4½″ × 4½″_

Total number of patches in block _21_

Number of different fabrics needed _3_

See the square forms illustrated below. Write in the total number needed of each in the space provided.

Total number of square forms[b] _9_

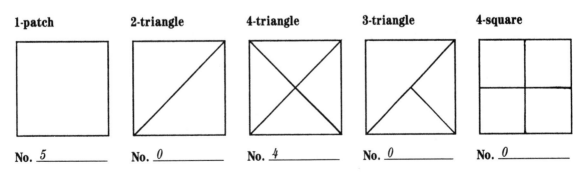

| 1-patch | 2-triangle | 4-triangle | 3-triangle | 4-square |
|---------|------------|------------|------------|----------|
| No. _5_ | No. _0_ | No. _4_ | No. _0_ | No. _0_ |

[a] Finished size of block is 12″ × 12″.
[b] Total number of squares and total number of square forms must be the same.

# Color Blocks Beautiful

**Name of block design:** _Ohio Star_

| Swatched square form[a] | How many in block design? | Placement in block design (square numbers) |
|---|---|---|
| | 4 | #2, 4, 6, 8 |
| | 1 | #5 |
| (Muslin) | 4 | #1, 3, 7, 9 |

[a] Duplicate each square in the block design that *differs* from the others in form and/or color. (Use additional pages as necessary.)

# Square Things Away

**Name of block design:** _Ohio Star_

Look carefully at the block design illustrated in Look and See. The chart below indicates what you are to look for. Write down what you see in the spaces that are provided. Read each column heading carefully and double-check your counting.

| Square form | Number of whole-cloth squares in block design, by fabric | Number of squares to cut, by fabric | Cutting size, of squares, by fabric[a] |
|---|---|---|---|
| **Whole-cloth** | Fabric A _1_ | _1_ | _4½″ × 4½″_ |
| | Fabric B _____ | _____ | _____ |
| | Fabric C (Muslin) _4_ | _4_ | _4½″ × 4½″_ |
| **Number in block design** _5_ | | | |

[a] Cutting size = finished size + ½″ for whole-cloth squares.

| Square form | Number of triangles in 4-triangle squares, by fabric | Number of squares to cut, by fabric[b] | Cutting size of squares, by fabric[c] |
|---|---|---|---|
| **4-triangle** | Fabric A _8_ | _2_ | _5⅜″ × 5⅜″_ |
| 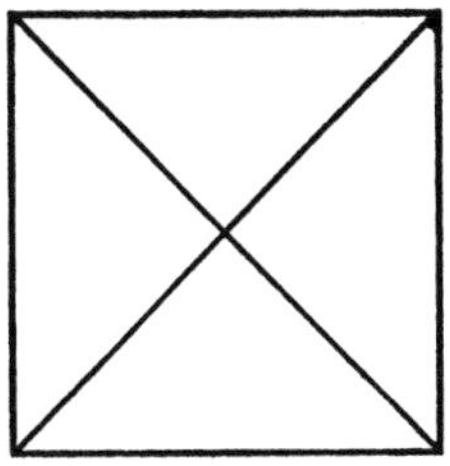 | Fabric B _4_ | _1_ | _5⅜″ × 5⅜″_ |
| | Fabric C (Muslin) _4_ | _1_ | _5⅜″ × 5⅜″_ |
| **Number in block design** _4_ | | | |

[b] Number of triangles divided by 4 = number of squares to cut. A full square is required for any number of triangles less than 4.
[c] Cutting size = finished size + 1⅜″.

# Tie It All Together: A Summary Chart for Cutting

**Name of block design:** _Ohio Star_

| Which fabrics? | Fabric swatch[a] | How many squares? | How big? | Patch form involved? |
|---|---|---|---|---|
| A | | 1 | $4\frac{1}{2}'' \times 4\frac{1}{2}''$ | 1-Patch |
| | | 2 | $5\frac{3}{8}'' \times 5\frac{3}{8}''$ | 4-Triangle |
| | | | | |
| B | | 1 | $5\frac{3}{8}'' \times 5\frac{3}{8}''$ | 4-Triangle |
| | | | | |
| | | | | |
| C (Muslin) | | 4 | $4\frac{1}{2}'' \times 4\frac{1}{2}''$ | 1-Patch |
| | | 1 | $5\frac{3}{8}'' \times 5\frac{3}{8}''$ | 4-Triangle |
| | | | | |

[a] Color or paste in the fabric swatches identified in Look and See.

## Completed Planning Charts for Louisiana

The completed Louisiana charts are based on my model, shown in the color section (color page H).

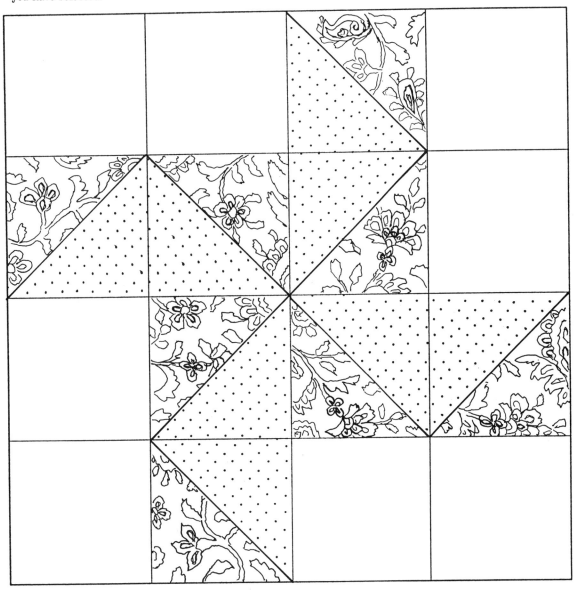

### Choose a Design: 16 Squares

This illustration serves as a kind of road map. It shows you *where* you are going. It tells you *when* you get there. Duplicate the design you wish to construct within the reduced block form. Color or paste in swatches of the fabrics you have selected.

**Name of block design:** *Louisiana*

# Look and See (Form and Color): 16 Squares

Name of block design: _Louisiana_

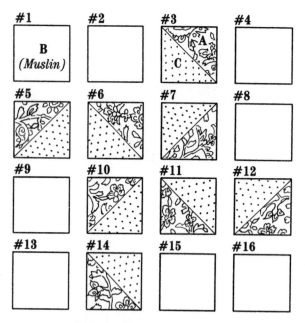

- Draw in the design you wish to construct.
- Color or paste in swatches of your chosen fabrics.
- Number the squares 1 to 16 from left to right and top to bottom.
- Letter the fabrics A, B, C, D, etc.

# List All the Givens (Basic Information)

Name of block design: _Louisiana_

Study the design presented in Choose a Design and complete the following blanks:

Finished size of block design _12″ × 12″_

Total number of squares in block[a] _16_

Finished size of each square _3″ × 3″_

Total number of patches in block _24_

Number of different fabrics needed _3_

See the square forms illustrated below. Write in the total number needed of each in the space provided.

Total number of square forms[a] _16_

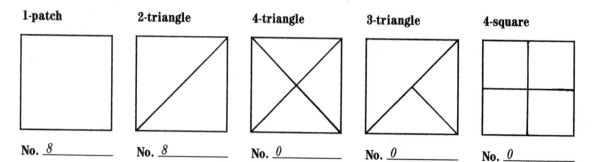

| 1-patch | 2-triangle | 4-triangle | 3-triangle | 4-square |
|---|---|---|---|---|
| No. _8_ | No. _8_ | No. _0_ | No. _0_ | No. _0_ |

[a] Total number of squares and total number of square forms must be the same.

76

# Color Blocks Beautiful

**Name of block design:** _Louisiana_

| Swatched square form[a] | How many in block design? | Placement in block design (square numbers) |
|---|---|---|
| | _8_ | _#3,5,6,7,10,11,12,14_ |
| _(Muslin)_ | _8_ | _#1,2,4,8,9,13,15,16_ |

[a] Duplicate each square in the block design that _differs_ from the others in form and/or color. (Use additional pages as necessary.)

# Square Things Away

**Name of block design:** _Louisiana_

Look carefully at the block design illustrated in Look and See. The chart below indicates what you are to look for. Write down what you see in the spaces that are provided. Read each column heading carefully and double-check your counting.

| Square form | Number of whole-cloth squares in block design, by fabric | Number of squares to cut, by fabric | Cutting size, of squares, by fabric |
|---|---|---|---|
| Whole-cloth | Fabric A _____ | _____ | _____ |
| | Fabric B __8__ (Muslin) | _____8_____ | _3½" × 3½"_ |
| | Fabric C _____ | _____ | _____ |

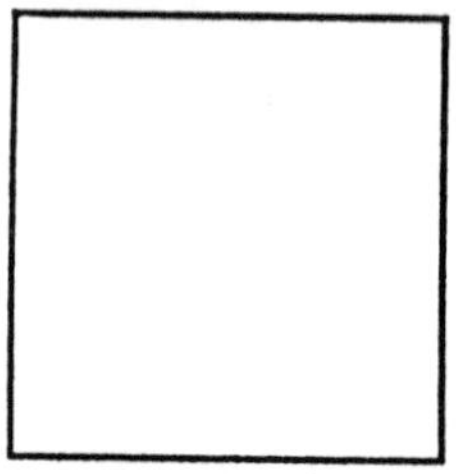

**Number in block design __8__**

| Square form | Number of triangles from 2-triangle squares, by fabric | Number of squares to cut, by fabric[a] | Cutting size of squares, by fabric |
|---|---|---|---|
| 2-triangle | Fabric A __8__ | _____4_____ | _3⅞" × 3⅞"_ |
| 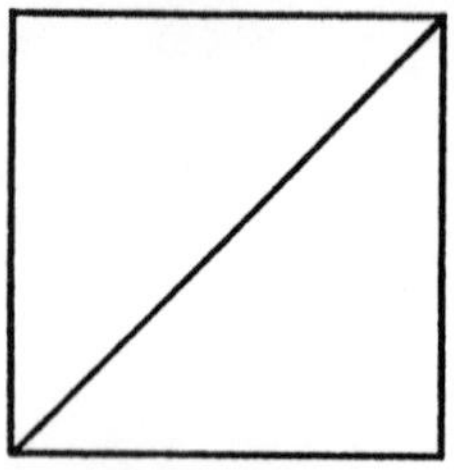 | Fabric B _____ (Muslin) | _____ | _____ |
| | Fabric C __8__ | _____4_____ | _3⅞" × 3⅞"_ |

**Number in block design __8__**

[a] Number of triangles divided by 2 = number of squares to cut. A full square is required for any number of triangles less than 2.

# Tie It All Together: A Summary Chart for Cutting

**Name of block design:** _Louisiana_

| Which fabrics? | Fabric swatch[a] | How many squares? | How big? | Patch form involved? |
|---|---|---|---|---|
| A | | 4 | 3⅞″ × 3⅞″ | 2-Triangle |
| B (Muslin) | | 8 | 3½″ × 3½″ | 1-Patch |
| C | | 4 | 3⅞″ × 3⅞″ | 2-Triangle |

[a] Color or paste in the fabric swatches identified in Look and See.

## Completed Planning Charts for
## Card Tricks

The completed Card Tricks charts are based on my
model, shown in the color section (color page G).

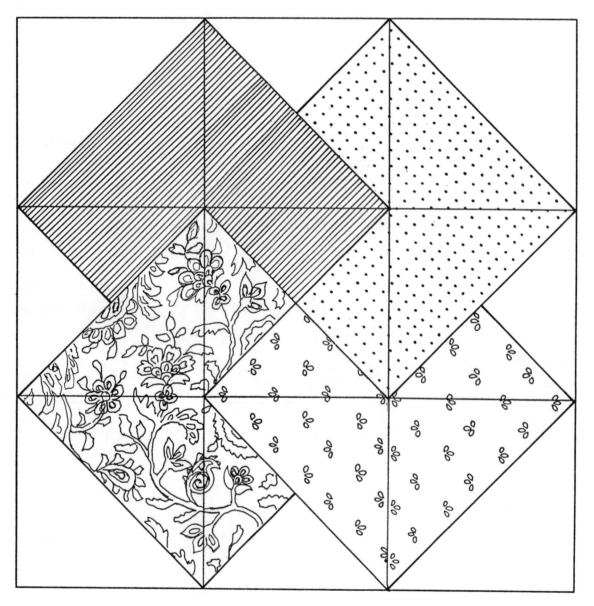

### Choose a Design: 9 Squares

This illustration serves as a kind of road map. It shows you *where* you are going. It tells you *when* you get there.
Duplicate the design you wish to construct within the reduced block form. Color or paste in swatches of the fabrics
you have selected.

**Name of block design:** _Card Tricks_

# Look and See (Form and Color): 9 Squares

**Name of block design:** _Card Tricks_

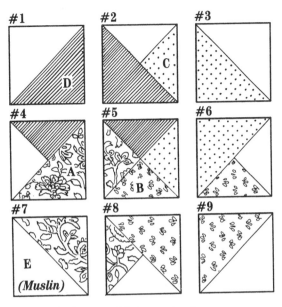

- Draw in the design you wish to construct.
- Color or paste in swatches of your chosen fabrics.
- Number the squares 1 to 9 from left to right and top to bottom.
- Letter the fabrics A, B, C, D, etc.

# List All the Givens (Basic Information)

**Name of block design:** _Card Tricks_

Study the design presented in Choose a Design and complete the following blanks:

Finished size of block design _12″ × 12″_
Total number of squares in block[a] _9_
Finished size of each square _4″ × 4″_
Total number of patches in block _24_
Number of different fabrics needed _5_

See the square forms illustrated below. Write in the total number needed of each in the space provided.

Total number of square forms _9_

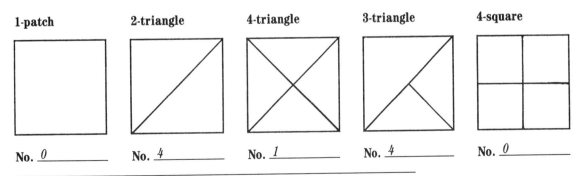

| 1-patch | 2-triangle | 4-triangle | 3-triangle | 4-square |
|---|---|---|---|---|
| No. _0_ | No. _4_ | No. _1_ | No. _4_ | No. _0_ |

[a] Total number of squares and total number of square forms must be the same.

# Color Blocks Beautiful

**Name of block design:** _Card Tricks_

| Swatched square form[a] | How many in block design? | Placement in block design (square numbers) |
|---|---|---|
| | 1 | #3 |
| | 1 | #9 |
| | 1 | #1 |
| | 1 | #7 |

## Color Blocks Beautiful, Card Tricks, continued

| Swatched square form[a] | How many in block design? | Placement in block design (square numbers) |
|---|---|---|
| | 1 | #5 |
| | 1 | #6 |
| | 1 | #2 |
| | 1 | #8 |
| | 1 | #4 |

[a] Duplicate each square in the block design that *differs* from the others in form and/or color. (Use additional pages as necessary.)

# Square Things Away

**Name of block design:** _Card Tricks_

Look carefully at the block design illustrated in Look and See. The chart below indicates what you are to look for. Write down what you see in the spaces that are provided. Read each column heading carefully and double-check your counting.

| Square form | Number of triangles from 2-triangle squares, by fabric[a] | Number of squares to cut, by fabric[a] | Cutting size of squares, by fabric |
|---|---|---|---|
| 2-triangle | Fabric A _1_ | _1_ | $4\frac{7}{8}'' \times 4\frac{7}{8}''$ |
| | Fabric B _1_ | _1_ | $4\frac{7}{8}'' \times 4\frac{7}{8}''$ |
| | Fabric C _1_ | _1_ | $4\frac{7}{8}'' \times 4\frac{7}{8}''$ |
| | Fabric D _1_ | _1_ | $4\frac{7}{8}'' \times 4\frac{7}{8}''$ |
| Number in block design _4_ | Fabric E _4_ | _4_ | $4\frac{7}{8}'' \times 4\frac{7}{8}''$ |

[a] Number of triangles divided by 2 = number of squares to cut. A full square is required for any number of triangles less than 2. Construction of this learning block is easier if a separate square is cut for each triangle appearing therein.

| Square form | Number of triangles from 4-triangle squares, by fabric | Number of squares to cut, by fabric[b] | Cutting size of squares, by fabric |
|---|---|---|---|
| 4-triangle | Fabric A _1_ | _1_ | $5\frac{3}{8}'' \times 5\frac{3}{8}''$ |
| | Fabric B _1_ | _1_ | $5\frac{3}{8}'' \times 5\frac{3}{8}''$ |
| | Fabric C _1_ | _1_ | $5\frac{3}{8}'' \times 5\frac{3}{8}''$ |
| | Fabric D _1_ | _1_ | $5\frac{3}{8}'' \times 5\frac{3}{8}''$ |
| Number in block design _1_ | Fabric E _0_ (Muslin) | _0_ | _0_ |

[b] Number of triangles divided by 4 = number of squares to cut. A full square is required for any number of triangles less than 4. Construction of this learning block is easier if a separate square is cut for each triangle appearing therein.

## Square Things Away, Card Tricks, continued

| Square form | Number of triangles from 1-triangle half of squares, by fabric | Number of squares to cut, by fabric[c] | Cutting size of squares, by fabric |
|---|---|---|---|
| **3-triangle** | | | |
| | Fabric A __1__ | __1__ | __$4\frac{7}{8}'' \times 4\frac{7}{8}''$__ |
| | Fabric B __1__ | __1__ | __$4\frac{7}{8}'' \times 4\frac{7}{8}''$__ |
| | Fabric C __1__ | __1__ | __$4\frac{7}{8}'' \times 4\frac{7}{8}''$__ |
| | Fabric D __1__ | __1__ | __$4\frac{7}{8}'' \times 4\frac{7}{8}''$__ |
| **Number in block design __4__** | Fabric E __0__ | __0__ | __0__ |

[c] Number of triangles divided by 2 = the number of squares to cut for the 1-triangle half. A full square is required for any number of triangles less than 2. Construction of this learning block is easier if a separate square is cut for each triangle appearing therein.

| Square form | Number of triangles in 2-triangle half of squares, by fabric | Number of squares to cut, by fabric[d] | Cutting size of squares, by fabric |
|---|---|---|---|
| **3-triangle** | | | |
| | Fabric A __1__ | __1__ | __$5\frac{3}{8}'' \times 5\frac{3}{8}''$__ |
| | Fabric B __1__ | __1__ | __$5\frac{3}{8}'' \times 5\frac{3}{8}''$__ |
| | Fabric C __1__ | __1__ | __$5\frac{3}{8}'' \times 5\frac{3}{8}''$__ |
| | Fabric D __1__ | __1__ | __$5\frac{3}{8}'' \times 5\frac{3}{8}''$__ |
| **Number in block design __4__** | Fabric E __4__ (Muslin) | __4__ | __$5\frac{3}{8}'' \times 5\frac{3}{8}''$__ |

[d] Number of triangles divided by 4 = number of squares to cut for the 2-triangle half. A full square is required for any number of triangles less than 4. Construction of this learning block is easier if a separate square is cut for each triangle appearing therein.

# Tie It All Together: A Summary Chart for Cutting

**Name of block design:** _Card Tricks_

| Which fabrics? | Fabric swatch[a] | How many squares? | How big? | Patch form involved? |
|---|---|---|---|---|
| A |  | _2_ | _4⅞" × 4⅞"_ | _2-Triangle and 3-Triangle[b]_ |
| | | _2_ | _5⅜" × 5⅜"_ | _3-Triangle[c] and 4-Triangle_ |
| | | | | |
| B | 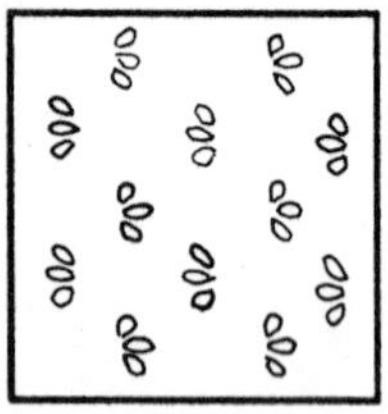 | _2_ | _4⅞" × 4⅞"_ | _2-Triangle and 3-Triangle[b]_ |
| | | _2_ | _5⅜" × 5⅜"_ | _3-Triangle[c] and 4-Triangle_ |
| | | | | |
| C | 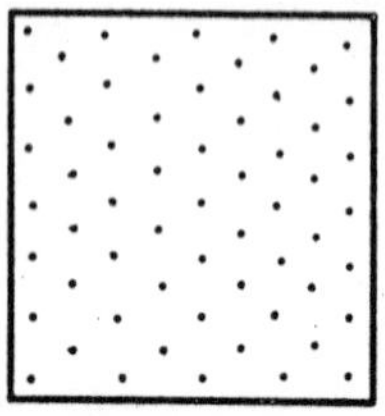 | _2_ | _4⅞" × 4⅞"_ | _2-Triangle and 3-Triangle[b]_ |
| | | _2_ | _5⅜" × 5⅜"_ | _3-Triangle[c] and 4-Triangle_ |
| | | | | |
| D |  | _2_ | _4⅞" × 4⅞"_ | _2-Triangle and 3-Triangle[b]_ |
| | | _2_ | _5⅜" × 5⅜"_ | _3-Triangle[c] and 4-Triangle_ |
| | | | | |
| E (Muslin) | | _4_ | _4⅞" × 4⅞"_ | _2-Triangle_ |
| | | _4_ | _5⅜" × 5⅜"_ | _3-Triangle[c]_ |
| | | | | |

[a] Color or paste in the fabric swatches identified in Look and See.
[b] From the 1-triangle half.
[c] From the 2-triangle half.

# —5—

# Making the
# Learning Blocks

## Introduction

Ready? Get set! Go! The process of patchworking is presented in a series of simple steps which I believe are easy to understand and follow. These steps are arranged in consecutive order and grouped according to the larger tasks or goals they are designed to accomplish. All of the how-to's necessary to complete each step are given before you move into the next. I suggest you read the entire chapter from start to finish several times *before* you *do* anything (except read and reflect on the words you read).

As you browse through the chapter for the first time, look at the format of presentation, think about patchwork as such—how it came to be, what you want the patchwork you do to look like. Instead of losing yourself in a taxing effort to absorb all the little details of doing (they will seem endless at this point), concentrate on the overall process in terms of the larger tasks to be accomplished—cutting, marking, stitching, assembly, etc. The doing will be easier and thus more pleasurable as a result of this kind of overview.

Once the first reading is completed, go back and read through the steps a second time. The how-to's will have greater impact during a second reading, so give your full attention this time to the *details* for completing the tasks.

This brings you up to the "read, then do" or work-through construction of a specific block design. This doing cycle is repeated until all of the learning blocks are finished and beautiful. By then you will have become a full-fledged patchworker who simply can't wait to begin the eighteen heirloom designs vying for attention in Chapter 6.

With all of this in mind, you are finally ready to learn to do patchwork by doing patchwork—six different learning designs that will provide a guided learning experience in every construction skill necessary to create beautiful patchwork. Easy? Yes! Fun? Yes! But there *are* conditions: (1) Complete all six of the designs in the order as presented; and (2) listen to and follow every single word of instruction precisely. Each design was carefully chosen to teach a specific skill that makes the doing of successive designs easier, thus the importance of the sequence.

The work-through is illustrated by one of the earliest known designs, the Nine-Patch. The simplicity of this old-fashioned pattern for a square quilt allows you to concentrate on the basic skills of cutting, marking, stitching, and assembly.

The process of sew easy is presented here in a series of steps that include the components you will need to make six learning blocks. The learning blocks (in the order of presentation) are: Nine-Patch, Hourglass, Susannah, Ohio Star, Louisiana, and Card Tricks. These are illustrated in color in the color section of the book and in Figure 10.

As you move through the consecutive listing of the doing steps, specific how-to's are often given for further clarification of the general instructions (those that are applicable for *every* design). These specifics, usually illustrations, are presented separately for the individual designs as necessary. The names of the designs in question are so noted. Supporting references for further enlargement of the how-to procedures are given throughout the construction process.

While this "inclusion" method of presentation was designed to eliminate repetitious writing of the general instructions for six different designs (*my* benefit), it creates a more important plus for *you*—repetitious reading—and repetition is always an excellent reinforcement for learning.

Please note that you don't actually begin to make your first block, the Nine-Patch block, until page 92, after you have studied the steps in general. You should proceed to make the learning blocks in order after you have completed the Nine-Patch, planning,

measuring, cutting, and assembling each one in its turn.

## Review of Necessary Steps

Now our task is to change paper planning into *patchworking. Perfect Patchwork* is designed to serve as a kind of workbook or guided learning experience in all of the various skills of patchworking. Therefore, the six learning blocks were already chosen and planned on paper in Chapter 4. These are now offered as "how-to" examples for both planning *and* doing. The following are general steps that pertain to all blocks.

*Step 1.* Review the General Plan in Chapter 4 from "start" through "put all your plans on paper" (page 44). Make certain that *everything* in the plan is in good order thus far. If it isn't, review the how-to references listed below and bring them up to date.

- Block design is chosen? (page 44).
- Fabrics are selected? (page 40).
- Swatched paste-up is ready? (page 40).
- All needed supplies (including fabrics) purchased? (pages 41–42).
- Horizontal and vertical grainlines established? (page 41).

**Nine-Patch**

**Hourglass**

*10. The six learning blocks (above and on page 89).*

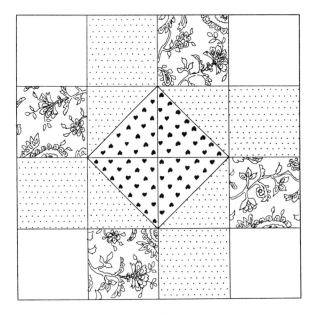

**Susannah**

Louisiana

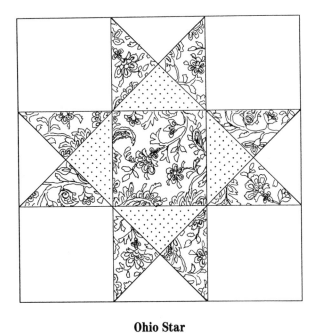

**Ohio Star**

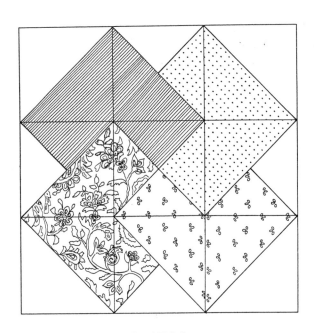

**Card Tricks**

- Fabrics straightened? Washed? Pressed? (page 41).

- All plans properly recorded on paper? (see charts in Chapter 4).

*Step 2.* Examine the format or layout for planning as a process by reviewing the six charts in Chapter 4 (pages 45–50). Make a deliberate effort to see planning as a logical part of doing. As you study these charts, look for the elements of planning discussed in Chapter 4. Pay special attention to the stated purpose for each individual chart, the way they evolve or grow out of those that precede, the interdependence of the activities they require. Think about the collective worth or expected end results of the information requested.

This kind of critical analysis provides greater insight into the process of doing. As a result, your perception of patchworking becomes one of unlimited opportunity for creative activity.

*Step 3.* Review the specific plan for the block design under construction. The completed planning charts for the six learning blocks are all given in Chapter 4. The completed plan for the learning block in progress serves as a how-to example for this particular patchworking skill. A plan for a specific design consists of a series of six information-gathering charts, which provide essential facts necessary to move you into doing with feelings of confidence. Read the charts with deliberate care in the sequence presented: Choose a Design, Look and See, List All the Givens, Color Blocks Beautiful, Square Things Away, and Tie It All Together.

*Step 4.* Make a duplicate working copy of four of the *blank* planning forms appearing in the Appendix of this book. They are: Choose a Design, Look and See, Color Blocks Beautiful, and Tie It All Together. These four forms provide a summary of essential reference information for the steps involved in doing.

*Step 5.* Go back to Chapter 4 and transfer all of the numerical information from the completed forms for the learning block design you wish to make to the corresponding blank forms that you have just copied. Double-check your working copies against the original plan to avoid any errors in transferring information.

*Step 6.* Using the swatched paste-up (Choose a Design) from Chapter 4 as a doing model, paste swatches of the fabrics *you* have selected in the appropriate spaces on the blank planning forms you have just prepared. This visible record of fabric selection and color distribution says very clearly that my "playing" plan has now become your working plan—one that will serve as a doing reference from this point forward. As you move through the how-to instructions, you will continue to substitute the fabrics shown in *your* working plan for those I

have used as teaching/learning examples in *my* playing plan.

*Step 7.* Reread the brief overview of the techniques of sew-easy patchworking given in Chapter 3 (page 16). This will help you better understand the entire procedure as you move through it. Remember that in sew-easy construction, all pieced squares begin as whole-cloth squares cut in preplanned colors and sizes that vary according to the patch form you wish to construct. The patch arrangement is drawn directly on one of two paired squares, which are then stitched together *before* they are cut into the small shapes drawn thereon. The resulting patch units ("units" because two squares of fabric have already been sewn together) are color-matched and stitched together to form the pieced squares necessary to make up the total block design.

## Cutting Squares Accurately

*Step 8.* Next we will cut the squares as indicated for the block design in progress. (See your working copy of the planning chart Tie It All Together and Table 11.) Instead of using a template for the squares in any given block design, for sew-easy patchwork the finished size plus seam allowances is measured from both grainline edges, marked off, and cut. The suggestions that follow are important to the accuracy of this first real doing step. Read them carefully before you cut the first square.

- Place a see-through quilter's ruler perpendicular to the grainline edge from which you wish to measure first.
- Align the required marking on the ruler parallel with the horizontal and/or vertical grainline edge and mark off the squares to be cut.
- Do not include the ravelled portion of a torn edge in your measurement. It isn't necessary that these ravels be cut away. Just remember to compensate for them when you mark the ¼" seam allowance!
- Be very careful that the desired crosswise mark on the ruler is *parallel* to the edge from which you are measuring.
- Note that the vertical edge of the ruler *may not be* parallel to the opposite grainline. This indicates that the fabric is off-grain (not perfectly straight), in which case the cut squares appear a little askew. Don't panic! It is easier to straighten a

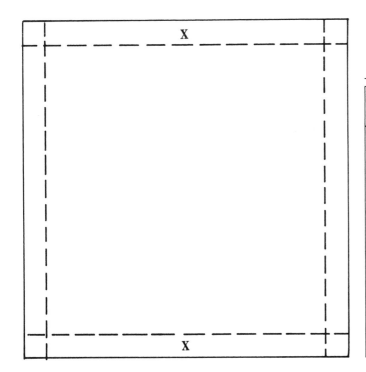

*11. Diagram of 3½″ square. Dashed line indicates seamline. X indicates crosswise direction of fabric. All markings are made on the wrong side of the fabric. The crosswise grain will stretch. The lengthwise grain will not.*

**Table 11a. Cutting Size for Whole-Cloth Squares for Sew-Easy Designs with 9 Squares**

| Square form | Size of whole cloth it is cut from |
|---|---|
| 1-patch | 4½″ × 4½″ |
| 2-triangle | 4⅞″ × 4⅞″ |
| 4-triangle | 5⅜″ × 5⅜″ |
| 3-triangle | |
| ◿ 1-triangle half | 4⅞″ × 4⅞″ |
| ◺ 2-triangle half | 5⅜″ × 5⅜″ |
| 4-square | 2½″ × 5″ |

**Table 11b. Cutting Size for Whole-Cloth Squares for Sew-Easy Designs with 16 Squares**

| Square form | Size of whole-cloth square it is cut from |
|---|---|
| 1-patch | 3½″ × 3½″ |
| 2-triangle | 3⅞″ × 3⅞″ |
| 4-triangle | 4⅜″ × 4⅜″ |
| 3-triangle | |
| ◿ 1-triangle half | 3⅞″ × 3⅞″ |
| ◺ 2-triangle half | 4⅜″ × 4⅜″ |
| 4-square | 2″ × 4″ |

small square than an entire width of fabric! This will be explained in "Squaring the Squares" a bit later in this chapter.

*Step 9.* Group the cut squares according to size, color, and square form designation for ease in the marking and stitching, steps that will be explained next.

## Marking Outside Seamlines Accurately

*Step 10.* Mark ¼″ seam allowances around the outside edges of *every* square, as illustrated in Figure 11. Keep the squares grouped according to square form designations. "X" both crosswise grainline directions within the seam allowance to mark the crosswise grain. I cannot overemphasize the fact that accurate measurements are *essential* to ease of construction and finished good looks. Since seam allowances are only ¼″ wide, you have very little margin for error; therefore, precision is a must.

The suggestions that follow will insure the achievement of precision if you follow them, so don't lift a pencil until you read and understand them.

- Align the ¼″ vertical marking of the see-through quilter's ruler with the cut edge of the square.
- Hold the ruler firmly against the fabric to prevent movement or shifting of fabric while marking.
- Keep your pencil sharp! Then your markings will be closer to the ruler, therefore more accurate.
- Hold pencil at 45° angle to the ruler. This brings you still closer to the edge.
- With lighter pressure on the pencil, mark the ¼″ seam allowance with long steady strokes.
- Mark from left to right or top to bottom, depending on angle of fabric to you. This helps to prevent movement of the fabric.
- Place the vertical marking of the ruler on the "off" side of the edges to compensate for possible inaccuracy.
- Be your own best critic. Check the seam widths: are they ¼″? Yes? No? If "no," why not? Review all the above (experience helps).

*Step 11.* When you have marked the seam allowances around the outside edges of all the squares you have cut for the design under construction, lay the 1-patch square forms (those to be used as whole-cloth squares within the design) aside until the pieced squares are completed. The number and unfinished size of the 1-patch or whole-cloth squares to cut for the learning blocks is noted in Table 12. The squares that remain after you separate your 1-patch squares are those required to construct the *pieced* squares for the design in progress. These squares may vary in both size and color, so I caution you again to keep them grouped and labelled. The steps upcoming will be easier and less confusing as a result.

## Laying Out and Stitching Up the Squares: Nine Patch

*Step 12.* Our next step will be to lay out, pin, and stitch the squares together to complete the design planned in the swatched paste-up.

- Lay the squares out to duplicate the design in the planning form Look and See given in Chapter 4.

### Table 12. Numbers and Sizes of 1-Patch Squares to Cut for the Learning Blocks

| Pattern | Number of Squares | Size of Square to Cut |
|---|---|---|
| Nine-Patch | 9 | 4½″ × 4½″ |
| Hourglass | 6 | 4½″ × 4½″ |
| Susannah | 12 | 3½″ × 3½″ |
| Ohio Star | 5 | 4½″ × 4½″ |
| Louisiana | 8 | 3½″ × 3½″ |
| Card Tricks | 0 | (None) |

- Lay out each square so that the crosswise grain-line of all the squares runs in the same direction, either up-down or left to right. We X'd the crosswise direction on the squares in Step 10. I usually lay out the crosswise grainline from left to right. The way you lay it out is not a critical matter, but consistency of direction *is* of critical importance to the final appearance of the Nine-Patch design. This is highly significant if your fabrics have a directional pattern, as is the case in some of the learning blocks models. (Also the fabric is stretchier on the crosswise grain than on the lengthwise grain.)
- Alignment will be difficult to achieve without some distortion if either or both squares are off-grain (see "Fabric Characteristics" in Chapter 1). Correct any lack of "squareness" before pinning the squares together for stitching as described next.
- To check the squareness of a square, lay each square against a right-angle corner: a tabletop, countertop, book cover, etc., and examine it carefully. If the each edge of a square is not parallel to an edge of the right angle, catch the offending corners and pull or stretch them gently in a bias grainline direction. Pressing lightly in this "pulling" direction may be an easier way to stabilize the straightened grain. The illustrations in Figure 12 will help to clarify these instructions.
- Pin and stitch the squares into rows as laid out in the Look and See chart. Check to be sure before you stitch each seamline that the pieces will open

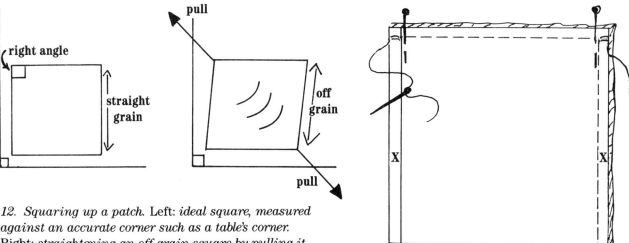

*12. Squaring up a patch.* Left: *ideal square, measured against an accurate corner such as a table's corner.* Right: *straightening an off-grain square by pulling it.*

*13. Pin two squares together for piecing and stitch across the top. Stitch from the outer edge of the seam allowances to the opposite edge, including the initial and final ¼".*

up to reveal the correct right-to-left relationship as is shown in your design. Align the cut edges, pin and stitch as is illustrated in figures 13, 14, and 15.

## The Piecing Stitch: All Blocks

The piecing stitch is a short running stitch, made with a single thread and secured with one or two small backstitches at the beginning and the end of the seam, which runs from cut edge to cut edge. Leave a tail of thread of at least 1″ at each end. (If you cut them too short you can't go back and make them any longer!) Pull very gently on the stitch to make certain that it *is* secure. See the Supplies List in Chapter 3 for the necessary sewing supplies. Uniformity of stitch length is important to the strength of the seam. Pull the thread through until it lies flat against the fabric. Avoid a tautness that "draws" or puckers the fabric.

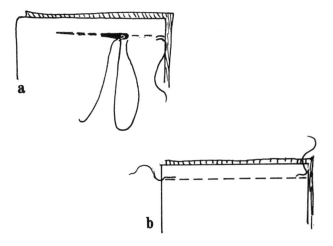

*14. a: Needle taking uniform-length stitches. b: Start and end each piecing with a stitch over a second stitch; don't use knots.*

## Joining the Squares Into Rows and the Rows Into Blocks

If you refer to the Look and See chart for any nine-square design, you'll realize that the first three squares (#1, 2, and 3) across, when joined, would form a row. The next three squares (#4, 5, and 6) will form the second row. The last three squares (#7, 8, and 9) will form the last row. To "build" our block, we will piece each square in a row to the one next to it, until we have three rows. After we make

the three rows, we will finger-press the seam allowances of each seam to one side. Then we'll join the rows together by stitching row 1 to row 2 all the way across, with right sides of fabric facing, using a ¼″ seam allowance. This basic building concept of joining squares into a row, and then joining rows into a block, applies to all the designs in this book; it will be used to create more complicated designs later on. (With 16-patch designs, each row has 4 blocks instead of 3, however.)

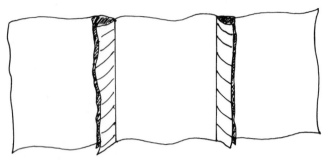

*15. Three squares sewn together in a row. Seam allowances were not pressed open.*

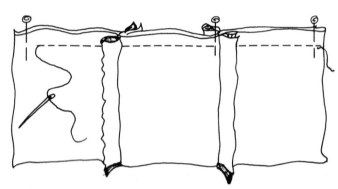

*16. Joining two rows. Vertical seam allowances are left free so they can be positioned well to minimize bulk later on (they are not sewn down).*

## Reviewing the Nine-Patch Block

Now that we've discussed the beginning cutting, marking, and piecing steps in general, it's time to put the knowledge you gained to work by making the first of the learning blocks, the Nine-Patch.

The Nine-Patch is among the oldest and most loved designs in patchwork. Though it is generally accepted as a beginner's block, it offers an unlimited potential for creative arrangements of color and pattern. The simplicity of this design (all nine of the squares are whole-cloth or one-patch square forms) provides an excellent learning opportunity for the basic skills of cutting, marking, pinning, stitching, finger-pressing, and assembly. This doing experience is designed to prepare you for a more detailed construction of the five remaining learning blocks, all of which contain pieced squares. First, plan your design, and get and prepare your fabric (refer to steps 1-7, pgs. 88–90). Then cut out and mark your nine squares, each measuring 4½″ × 4½″ (see steps 8 through 10, pgs. 90–92).

- Lay the squares out to duplicate the design in the planning form Look and See given in Chapter 4.

Be sure the grainline directions are correct and the pieces are square; correct if necessary.

- Piece the squares for row 1, row 2, and row 3 into the three rows (see above for details, including figures 14, 15 and 16).
- Finger-press the seam allowances on each seam. Finger-pressing is described in detail on pages 113–114.
- Pin and stitch row 1 to row 2, leaving already joined seam allowances free to move by passing your needle *under* the seam allowance (Figure 16).
- Join row 2 and row 3 in the same way.
- Press the block with seam allowances in alternating directions to minimize bulk (see p. 115).

## Pairing the Squares for Piecing: General Information

Next we'll learn how to pair and pin together the whole-cloth squares required to construct the *pieced* squares. This applies to any design you are doing that has squares that are made of more than 1 patch. Keep the paired squares labelled according to patch form.

Pairing the whole-cloth squares is a significant prerequisite to further marking and stitching. While it determines the distribution of pattern and color as planned, it also eliminates unnecessary marking, thereby reducing the probability of error. These factors contribute greatly to both ease and accuracy of construction, and *accuracy is a must* for the finished good looks of the patchwork you do.

As you look at the illustrations in preparation for the pairing procedure, think about two things in addition to the procedure itself. First, though the fabrics may differ for the same square form in different designs, the pairing procedure always remains exactly the same. Second, the data that appears in conjunction with the how-to's serves as a preliminary safeguard—a kind of check and balance system for the successful completion of this simple but influential doing step.

As you study the illustrations that follow, concern yourself only with the block design you are doing at the time. This lessens the likelihood of confusion, which is something that sew-easy patchworkers don't need.

## Pairing the Squares for the 2-Triangle Square Form

Combine whole-cloth squares cut from each of the two fabrics appearing in the 2-triangle square form. Table 13 has illustrations taken from the block designs in Chapter 4, showing 2-triangle squares. For 2-triangle square forms, the size of the whole-cloth squares to cut is equal to the size of the finished square unit plus ⅞″. By "square unit" I mean one of the 9 or 16 units that is pieced to make a block. All of the blocks in this book have a finished size of 12″ × 12″. Thus, for a 9-patch design, the size of the whole-

cloth square to cut is 4⅞″ × 4⅞″; that is, 12″ divided by 3 square units on the side of a 9-patch square = 4″; adding ⅞″ seam allowance this becomes 4⅞″. For a 16-patch block design each finished square unit = 3″ on a side (12″ divided by 4). Adding ⅞″, the size to cut for a 16-patch block design's 2-triangle square units is 3⅞″ × 3⅞″. Table 13 shows the learning blocks that have 2-triangle squares and shows which whole-cloth squares to pair up to piece the two-triangle square units. For a complicated design like Card Tricks, there are 4 different 2-triangle squares; a total of 8 whole-cloth squares is needed to make them. We'll discuss how to mark and piece the 2-triangle squares later in this chapter.

## Table 13. Whole-Cloth Squares (Pattern and Size) for 2-Triangle Square Forms in the Learning Blocks

| Block Design Name and 2-Triangle Square | 9- or 16-patch | Whole-Cloth Square Fabrics | | Size of Whole-Cloth Squares |
|---|---|---|---|---|
|  Hourglass | 9 |  |  | 4⅞″ × 4⅞″ each |
|  Susannah | 16 | 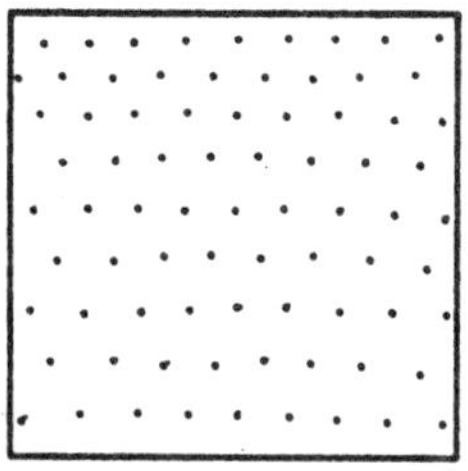 |  | 3⅞″ × 3⅞″ each |
|  Louisiana | 16 |  | 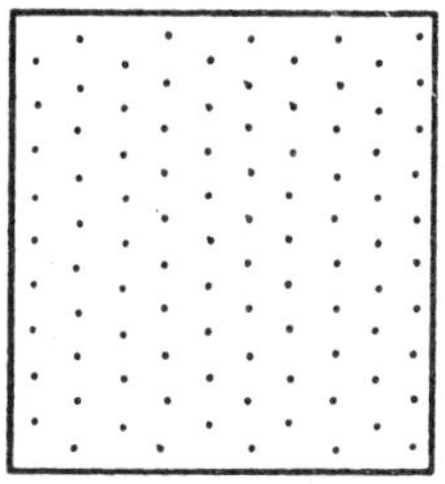 | 3⅞″ × 3⅞″ each |

**Table 13. Whole-Cloth Squares for 2-Triangle Square Forms, continued**

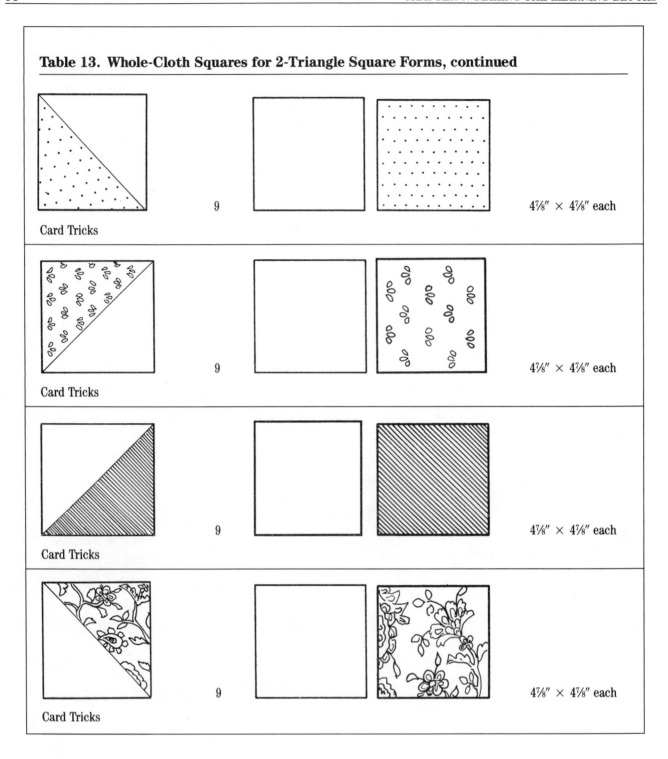

Card Tricks            9                                  4⅞″ × 4⅞″ each

Card Tricks            9                                  4⅞″ × 4⅞″ each

Card Tricks            9                                  4⅞″ × 4⅞″ each

Card Tricks            9                                  4⅞″ × 4⅞″ each

## Pairing the Squares for the 4-Triangle Square Form

For each triangle of the 4-triangle square form, a whole-cloth square is cut, each of which measures 5⅜″ × 5⅜″ (the finished size of the square [4″] +

1⅜″) in the learning blocks. Table 14 shows the 4-triangle squares needed for the learning blocks, and shows which whole-cloth squares to pair up in order to piece them. The fabrics are based on the models in the learning blocks. We'll discuss how to mark and piece the 4-triangle squares later in this chapter.

**Table 14. Whole-Cloth Squares for Making the 4-Triangle Square Forms in the Learning Blocks (9-Patch Size)**

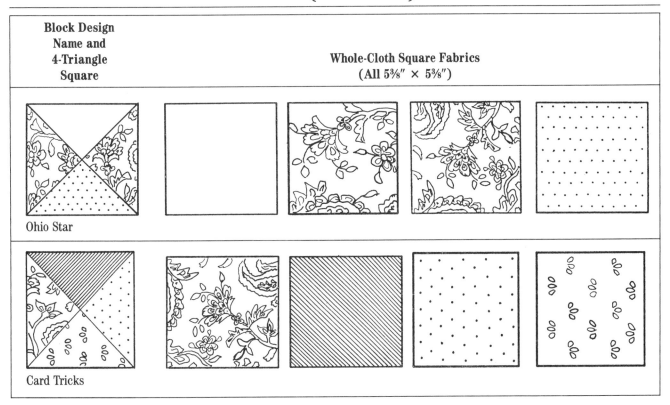

| Block Design Name and 4-Triangle Square | Whole-Cloth Square Fabrics (All 5⅜″ × 5⅜″) | | | |
|---|---|---|---|---|
| Ohio Star | | | | |
| Card Tricks | | | | |

## Pairing the Squares for the 3-Triangle Square Form

The 3-triangle square form has one large triangle and two small triangles. Cut one 5⅜″ whole-cloth square for each of the fabrics appearing in the two small triangles that form one-half of this square. Cut one 4⅞″ square for the large triangle that appears in the 3-triangle square form. The illustrations in Table 15 were taken from the Card Tricks learning block. Later we will discuss how to piece the squares. Be sure to keep the small (4⅞″) squares separate from the paired (5⅜″) squares.

## Pairing the Rectangles for the 4-Square Square Form

The 4-square square is created by using rectangles instead of squares. This unit occurs as the center of Hourglass. To make the 4-square square form, combine one rectangle from each of the two needed fabrics. For Hourglass, each rectangle measures 2½″ × 5″. The 5″ side should be cut on the crosswise grain of the fabric, as shown in Figure 17.

*17. A 4-square square form and the rectangles it is cut from. For Hourglass, each rectangle measures 2½″ × 5″.*

← CW →

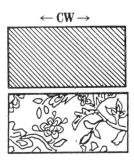

**Table 15.  Fabrics and Sizes of Whole-Cloth Squares to Cut for the
3-Triangle Squares in Card Tricks**

| Block Name: Card Tricks | Paired (5⅜") Squares for the Small Triangles | | Single (4⅞") Square for the Large Triangle |
|---|---|---|---|
| | | | |
| | | | |
| | | | |
| | | | |

## Marking the Squares for Piecing

As we saw in Pairing the Squares, each pieced square unit is made of two (or more) whole-cloth squares, joined together and then sewn and cut to the correct shape. Before we can join them, we need to mark their seamlines. Marking will be explained below, first in a general way.

In order to eliminate the repetition of specific instructions for marking the piecing squares, information that is applicable for five of the six learning blocks (except Nine-Patch, which has no pieced squares) is presented here.

Keep the following points in mind as you proceed with the marking procedure.

• The ¼" seam allowance is marked around the outside edges of *every square* and the square's crosswise grainlines are X'ed. You probably did this in Step 10, but check to see that you did.

• The *patch arrangement*, the *cutting lines* for eventual separation of the "patch units" and the *seamlines* for stitching these units together are marked on only one of the two paired squares. I usually choose the square on which the markings are easier to see, *except* in the instance of concern for grainline direction in a patterned fabric.

- The marking illustrations (figures 18, 19, and 20) are drawn full-scale, thereby giving you an opportunity for a quick and accurate sizing check. Just lay your whole-cloth square over the square as drawn. It should fit perfectly. (It must!)

- All markings are made on the wrong side of the fabric. You might like to go back at this point and reread the suggestions for accurate marking given earlier (pp. 91–92). This may be time well spent. Let's look now at the illustrations that are going to tell you how to mark these "piecing" squares.

Specific instructions for each square form are given in the sections that follow.

## Marking the Squares for the 2-Triangle Square Form

Take two whole-cloth squares for a 2-triangle square, like the ones in Susannah. Mark one of the two paired squares as follows (see Fig. 18 and 19):

- Draw a ¼″ seam allowance around the outside edges of each square; put X's on the fabrics' crosswise grains.

- Make one cutting line connecting two opposite corners on the diagonal. (Though this usually can be drawn from either direction, it is *designated* for Card Tricks to accommodate grainline direction of patterned fabrics.) Don't cut the triangles yet, however.

- Mark a ¼″ seam allowance on both sides of the diagonal cutting line. This will become the seam allowance when the squares are cut into triangles.

## Marking the Squares for the 4-Triangle Square Form

Take two paired whole-cloth squares for a 4-triangle square, like the ones in Ohio Star. Mark one of the two paired squares as follows (see Fig. 20):

- Draw a ¼″ seam allowance around the outside edges of each square; put X's on the crosswise grainlines of each square.

- Draw two cutting lines connecting the four oppo-

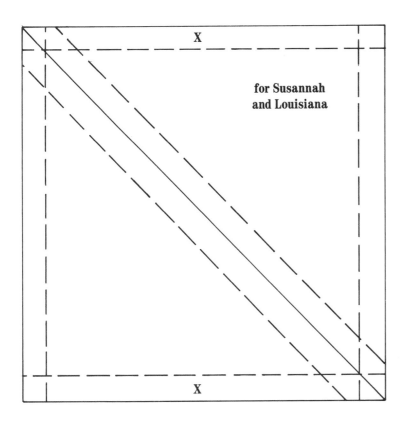

*18. Full-size marking diagram for 2-triangles squares from the 3⅞″ square. Dashed lines are stitching lines. Solid lines are cutting lines. X indicates crosswise grain of fabric.*

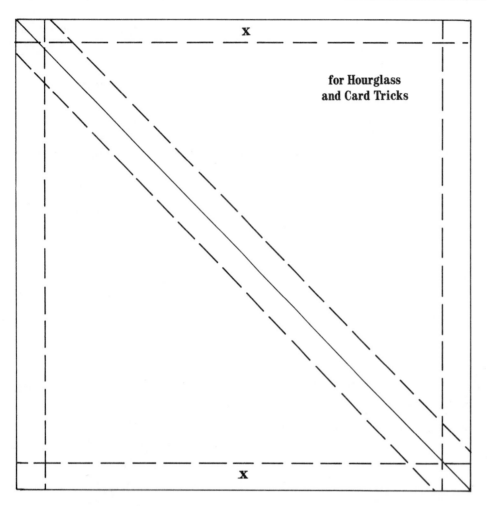

for Hourglass
and Card Tricks

x

x

*19. Full-size marking diagram for 2-triangle squares from the 4⅞" square. Dashed lines are stitching lines. Solid lines are cutting lines. X indicates crosswise grain of fabric.*

site corners on the diagonals, but don't cut the triangles yet.
• Draw a ¼" seam allowance on *both sides of each* cutting line. These will be the triangle's seam allowances.

## Marking the Squares for the 3-Triangle Square Form

The 3-triangle square form appears in only one of the learning blocks, Card Tricks. The marking patterns for both the 2-triangle and 4-triangle square are used to make the 3-triangle square form. See the pages preceding for marking directions. (The square in Fig. 21 is intended to serve as a "sizing check" for accuracy of measurements). The two-triangle square is used to make the large triangle. Mark the small-triangle half by using the 4-triangle square.

## Marking the Squares for the 4-Square Square Form

As discussed earlier, this form begins by cutting two rectangles, each 2½" × 5", when it is used in the Hourglass design. To mark the rectangle (Fig. 22):

• Mark ¼" seam allowances around the outside edge of one rectangle, as described earlier in Step 10.
• Draw a cutting line through the center of the rectangle as shown in Figure 22, forming two squares of equal size. Don't cut the squares yet, however.
• Mark ¼" seam allowances on both sides of the cutting line you just drew.

## Stitching Up the Pieced Squares

Next we will learn to construct the pieced squares without any visible indications of error.

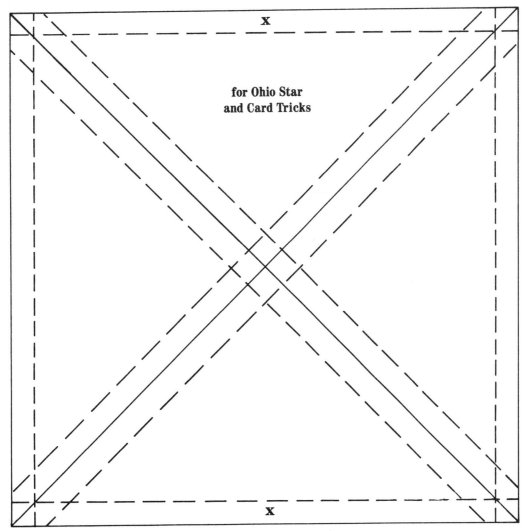

for Ohio Star
and Card Tricks

20. *Full-size marking diagram for making 4-triangle squares from 5⅜" squares. Dashed lines are stitching lines. Solid lines are cutting lines.*

## General Information

The following applies to all squares forms; specific cases will be discussed later on.

- Lay the two paired squares together with the right sides of fabric facing each other. The marked square, in either grainline direction, is placed *over* the second square, but in an opposing grainline direction (Fig. 23).
- Align the cut edges perfectly and pin the squares together as shown in Figure 24.
- Follow the general instructions for the "squaring" of an off-grain square.
- Stitch along the interior seamlines around the interior cut line *only* at this stage.

## Stitching Up the 2-Triangle Squares

Two-triangle squares occur in Hourglass, Susannah, and Louisiana in the learning blocks.

- Place the pins parallel to the grainline and about ½" inside the cut edge (Fig. 24).
- Place two pins near the seamline, but far enough away to avoid interference with stitching and/or cutting.
- Place the other two pins near the corners as shown.
- Stitch *only* along the seamlines on each side of the cut line at this point. This will yield two pieced squares.
- Cut along the cut line and open the pieced squares out (Fig. 25).

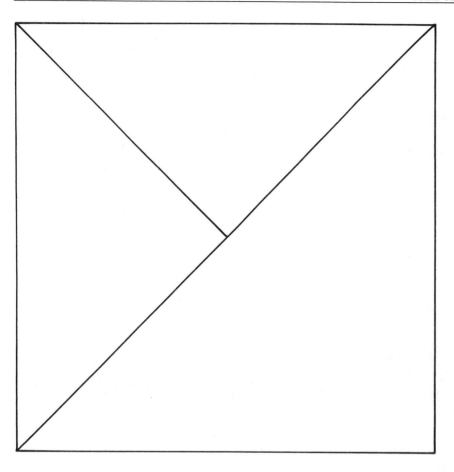

*21.  Final size, without seam allowances, of the 3-triangle square for Card Tricks.*

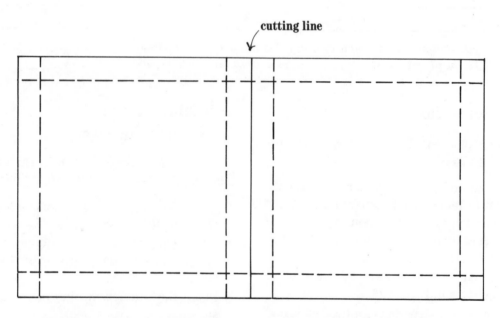

*22.  The rectangle used to make the 4-square square form. Mark ¼" seam allowances around the lighter of the two fabrics on the wrong side. Mark a cutting line, dividing the rectangle into two squares. Mark seamlines ¼" away from the cutting line. Dashed lines are seamlines.*

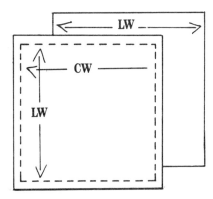

*23. The marked two-triangle square, in either grainline direction, is placed over the second square, but in an opposing grainline direction.*

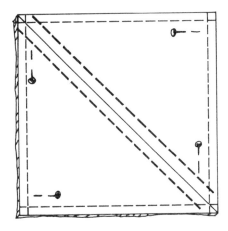

*24. Pinning and stitching guide for the 2-triangle square. Stitch only along the interior seamlines (heavy dashes) at this stage.*

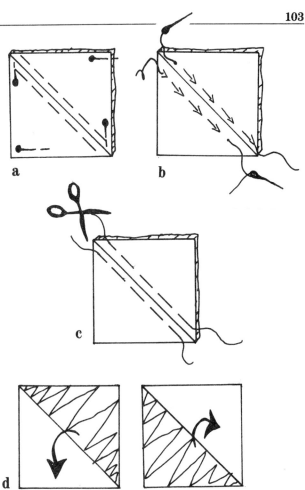

*25. Steps in pinning, cutting, and stitching a 2-triangle square. a: Two whole-cloth squares, pinned and marked. b: Stitch them together along the inner seamlines. c: Cut along the cut line. d: Open out into 2 pieced squares.*

## Stitching Up the 4-Triangle Squares

In the learning blocks, the 4-triangle square is needed for the Ohio Star and Card Tricks. Below we'll explain the process for the Ohio Star. See Figure 31 for the Card Tricks 4-triangle square.

- It takes four whole-cloth squares to construct the pieced 4-triangle squares in the Ohio Star. For our learning block model, you need two Fabric A squares, one Fabric C square, and one B square (muslin) (see Table 14, pg. 97).

- With right sides of fabric facing, place two paired squares together. (Check the swatched paste-up to see which). Make sure that they are laid in opposing grainline directions (see Figure 23).

- Align the cut edges carefully. If the squares were measured, cut, and marked accurately they will be the same size. This is a must! Any error is magnified as you progress through the "piecing" process.

- If the opposite corners show slightly, the squares may be a little off-grain despite your efforts to straighten the fabric itself earlier. Pull gently to straighten and realign them once more. They *must* be the same size, and also squared up.

- Pin the paired squares together as shown in Figure 26 and stitch on the seamlines (indicated with dashed lines on the figure).

- Stitch the seamlines on either side of the cut lines. You may find it easier to keep the squares properly aligned if you stitch from the center intersection out toward the corners. This will give you some-

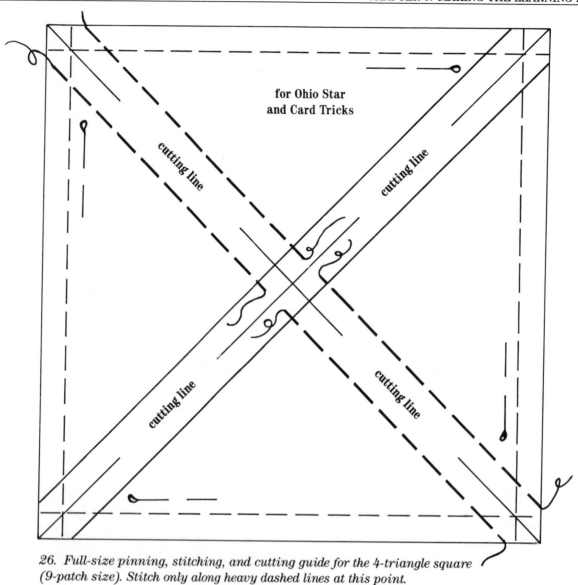

**for Ohio Star
and Card Tricks**

*cutting line* *cutting line* *cutting line* *cutting line*

26. *Full-size pinning, stitching, and cutting guide for the 4-triangle square
(9-patch size). Stitch only along heavy dashed lines at this point.*

thing to hold on to. Don't stitch *across* a cut line. Start a new thread on either side. Do not forget to begin and end with a small backstitch. See other stitching directions given earlier ("The Piecing Stitch" and Fig. 14).

• When the stitching is completed, cut the squares apart on both diagonal cutting lines (Fig. 26). Hold the tails of your stitching thread away from the scissors. (Here is where you need the trimming-size scissors.) Cutting through the center intersection of these seams requires extreme care to avoid cutting the ending stitches.

• Keep the pins in place so that the unstitched sections remain in perfect alignment while you are cutting. Do be very careful.

• Once the stitched squares are cut apart, there will

be eight small triangular units ("units" because the triangles are composed of two patches of fabric). In the case of Ohio Star, each is either a combination of Fabric A and Fabric C *or* Fabric A and Fabric B, as shown in Figure 27.

• These units are opened up into larger triangles. Each triangle will form half of one of the four pieced squares within the total design (see swatched paste-up for Ohio Star, page 70).

• Arrange the open triangles to duplicate the arrangement of the pieced squares in the swatched paste-up. Gently finger-press seams of the triangles in opposing directions (see Fig. 28 and 40) to reduce bulk at seam intersections. Matching seamlines will be easier and top surfaces will be smoother if you do this.

27. *Two pieced triangles cut from 4-triangle squares for the Ohio Star.*

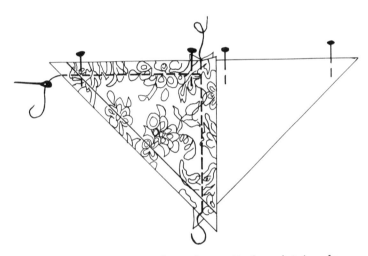

28. *Joining two triangular units for a 4-triangle square.*

- The longer edges are on the bias, so they must be handled with *extreme care* to avoid any stretching; stretching can mean difficulty in fitting patches and/or squares together later on.
- Lay the paired triangles together with right sides facing each other.
- Carefully align the center seams, cut edges, and corners. Pin as shown in Figure 28 and stitch them together. Note that seam allowances from the earlier joining are turned in opposing directions.
- It may be easier to keep the seams and edges aligned if you begin at the center seam and sew toward the corner. Turn the triangle over and complete the seam, working from the center out. (Remember to begin and end with a backstitch, leaving a tail of thread, and to hold the previously

joined seam allowances out of the way so that they are free.)

- Finger-press the seams carefully after stitching. Avoid turning them toward the lighter fabric, through which color may be seen from the upper side of the square.
- When opened out, the 4-triangle square will be formed.

## Stitching Up the 3-Triangle Squares

These are discussed in the next section in Card Tricks (see pages 107–110), so they will not be covered here.

## Stitching Up the 4-Square Squares

This unit is used in the learning blocks for Hourglass.

- Unlike the preceding square forms, the 4-square squares begin with two *rectangles* that differ in color and/or pattern.
- Check the grainlines of the rectangles. The longer sides (5″) should be on the *crosswise grain.*
- Lay these rectangles together with right sides of fabric facing. Align the edges and pin as shown in Figure 29a.
- Stitch the two vertical seamlines adjacent to the cutting line. Begin and end with a small backstitch, leaving short tails of thread at either end.
- Cut the two small squares apart on the indicated cutting line and open them up to form two rectangles. Each rectangle is made up of two small squares that differ in color and/or pattern.
- Arrange these to duplicate the 4-square square on the swatched paste-up for the Hourglass (page 60). Finger-press the seamlines in opposing directions.
- Lay the two rectangles together, with right sides facing. Pin and stitch them together from the center out, following the seamline markings, flip them over and stitch from the center out (Fig. 29c).

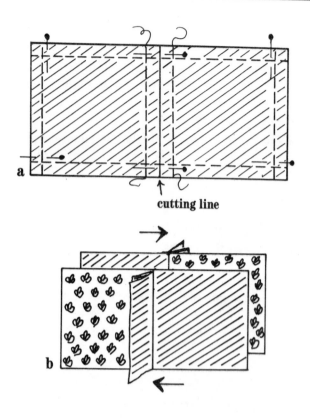

cutting line

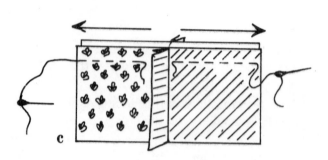

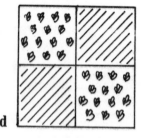

29.    a. *Stitching up two rectangles to make the 4-square square. b: Finger-press seamlines in opposite directions. c: Stitch from the center out on one marked seamline; flip the unit over and stitch on the other side to complete the piecing. d: The finished unit.*

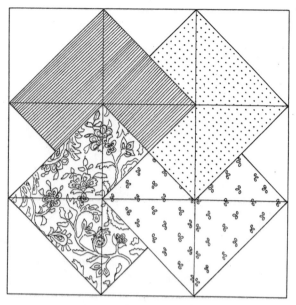

30.  *Card Tricks, swatched paste-up.*

# Perfectly Pieced Patchwork: Card Tricks

Our next task will be to relate color and pattern to grainline direction. We will learn to do this by marking, pinning and stitching the pieced squares appearing in the Card Tricks block. Card Tricks, the last learning block, a challenging but graphically beautiful design, is in reality a composite of all of the patchworking skills discussed heretofore, plus additional others that will be new to you. Look at the completed design in both the black-and-white sketch (Fig. 30) and on color page G. Every small square of the block is pieced; every square is different in both patch arrangement and color from the others. Furthermore the fabric's grainline direction in each little patch (there are 24 of them) is precisely matched to those of the same fabric in the adjacent patches. This doesn't just happen! It comes about as a result of thoughtful attention to detail; it isn't difficult to achieve with the techniques of sew easy.

Every step necessary to the piecing of perfect squares of patchwork within the Card Tricks block is illustrated on the pages following. All you have to do now is substitute your choices of fabric for A, B, C, and D plus muslin (E), and duplicate the diagrams presented for the square forms. You will need four 2-triangle squares, one 4-triangle square, and four 3-triangle squares (see Table 13 and 14).

The procedures for layout and marking give attention to the relationship of color and pattern to grainline direction. Neither of the three factors can be considered independently of the other, if you want to combine all 24 of the little patches to form four different wholes within the total design while still retaining the appearance of unity of design. So, I emphasize again, listen to the words and look at the doing diagrams and then duplicate them precisely. Remember too, that you are still learning, and that all of the designs hereafter will be sew easy, and beautiful, and fun to do!

Go back to Chapter 4 and, if you have not already done so, make a swatched paste-up of Card Tricks using the Choose a Design form and purchase, wash, and cut out your squares. The squares' sizes are indicated in the chart on page 86 (Tie It All Together).

You are ready at this point to piece the squares for Card Tricks. You will construct the 2-triangle squares first, the 4-triangle squares second, and then combine the two to provide the 3-triangle squares.

## 2-Triangle Squares for Card Tricks

- The pieced squares, as shown in Color Blocks Beautiful in Chapter 4 (p. 82), also appear in the left column of Table 16 (p. 108). These are the squares you are learning to duplicate. Refer to the Look and See chart (p. 81) for the square numbers.

- The paired squares from which the pieced squares are made appear in the second and third columns of Table 16. Place the patterned square in front of you first, right side up, with the grainline direction shown in column 2 of Table 16.

- To make the 2-triangle squares, lay the muslin square over the patterned square, wrong-side up, in an opposing grainline direction to the patterned square (see Table 16). "Opposing" here means the crosswise grain on the top square runs in the direction that the lengthwise grain runs on the bottom square.

- Both squares should have been marked around the outside edges in Step 10 (p. 91); if they were not, do so now.

- Next, mark the stitching and cutting lines on the muslin squares in a diagonal direction as is shown in Table 16. The general instructions for marking the stitching and cutting lines, given earlier (p. 99), are applicable, except for the direction of the

diagonal, which will differ for some of the squares in the Card Tricks design.

- Pin and stitch (pp. 101–103) the 2-triangle squares on both sides of the diagonal line, as was discussed in the general pinning and stitching instructions.

- If you are unable to determine the grainline direction visually (it is difficult in solid colors and muslin) remember that there is *some stretch* in the crosswise direction, but *none* in the lengthwise direction.

- Carefully cut the pieced triangle units apart along the diagonals you just marked.

- For assembling Card Tricks, use the half indicated by X in Table 16, column 3. Put the remaining half of each aside for later use.

## 4-Triangle Square for Card Tricks

The 4-triangle square to be duplicated for the center of Card Tricks appears in Figure 31. The grainline directions, shown with the square as it is oriented in the finished design, are noted thereon. The construction of the 4-triangle square is essentially the same as that of the Ohio Star (pp. 103–105).

- The required grainline layout is noted for each square in Figure 31. The fabrics, identified by letter, are based on the sample; see color page G.

- The diagonal seamlines to be stitched are noted in Figure 31 on the appropriate squares (B and D). Refer to Ohio Star 4-triangle square instructions for marking, stitching, and cutting (pp. 99, 103, 104).

- Only one of the triangular units in each of the paired squares is needed to make the Card Tricks 4-triangle square.

- The unit is marked with an X in Figure 31. Cut along the cut lines in Figure 31 to separate it, and set the others aside.

- Refer to the Ohio Star instructions to join the two pieced triangular units (p. 105) to complete the 4-triangle square.

## 3-Triangle Square for Card Tricks

Table 17 shows the instructional diagrams for this square form.

- The squares to be duplicated appear in the column to your left.

## Table 16.  Piecing the 2-Triangle Squares for Card Tricks

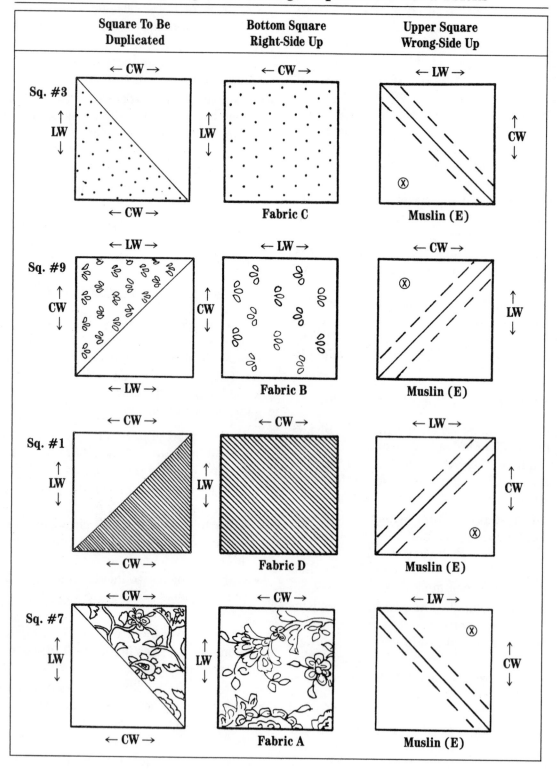

| Square To Be Duplicated | Bottom Square Right-Side Up | Upper Square Wrong-Side Up |
|---|---|---|
| Sq. #3 | Fabric C | Muslin (E) |
| Sq. #9 | Fabric B | Muslin (E) |
| Sq. #1 | Fabric D | Muslin (E) |
| Sq. #7 | Fabric A | Muslin (E) |

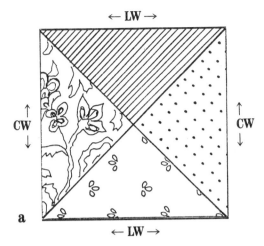

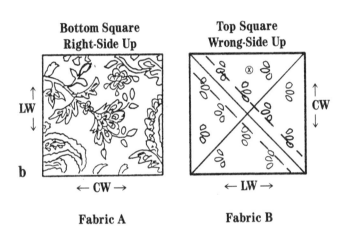

Bottom Square
Right-Side Up

Top Square
Wrong-Side Up

Fabric A          Fabric B

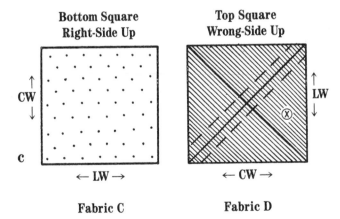

Bottom Square
Right-Side Up

Top Square
Wrong-Side Up

Fabric C          Fabric D

*31. a: A swatched 4-triangle square, the center of Card Tricks, based on the model. b and c: the two sets of two whole-cloth squares that are joined to make the triangles for the central 4-triangle square. ⊗ indicates the quarter that is used.*

- The left-hand square combines half of a 2-triangle square and half of a 4-triangle square as well. Each is numbered as in the Look and See chart on page 81.
- The grainline directions as you will view the squares in the completed design are noted.
- The construction the two-triangle half of the 3-triangle square duplicates that of the Ohio Star, but with these exceptions: Designation of grainline layout, designation of the diagonal seamlines to be stitched, and designation of the differing "units" used in both halves of the square. These are noted in Table 17.
- If you failed to identify the grainline of the squares as they were cut, just remember that the crosswise direction *is more flexible* (stretchier) and has some "give," while the lengthwise direction *is very stable* and without any "give."
- The diagonal seamlines to be stitched are indicated on the appropriate squares in Table 17, column 3, on the muslins. You probably marked these earlier.
- The triangular "units" which you are to use are marked with a circled X. Make certain that the grainline direction of the marked unit is the same as that of the unit shown in the third column of Table 17.
- Cut the X'ed "units" away from the stitched squares; open them up into a larger triangle; then finger-press the seam allowances toward the colored half of the triangles. Do this with extreme care to avoid even the slightest distortion or stretch!
- Lay the pieced triangle over the X'ed half of the whole-cloth square given in column 4 (Table 17), with right sides facing. The whole-cloth square should be 4⅞″ × 4⅞″.
- Pin and stitch the pieced triangle and the whole-cloth square together (Fig. 32). The center of the diagonal should be a matching point for the inner seam of the pieced triangle! Leave the whole-cloth square in its entirety during this process, then cut the extra half away after the pieced triangle and the whole-cloth square are stitched with right sides facing each other and seams aligning.
- Make the 3 other 3-triangle squares in the same way, following Table 17 for guidance.
- To assemble the Card Tricks block, see the next section, "Building the Blocks."

## Table 17.  Piecing the 3-Triangle Squares for Card Tricks

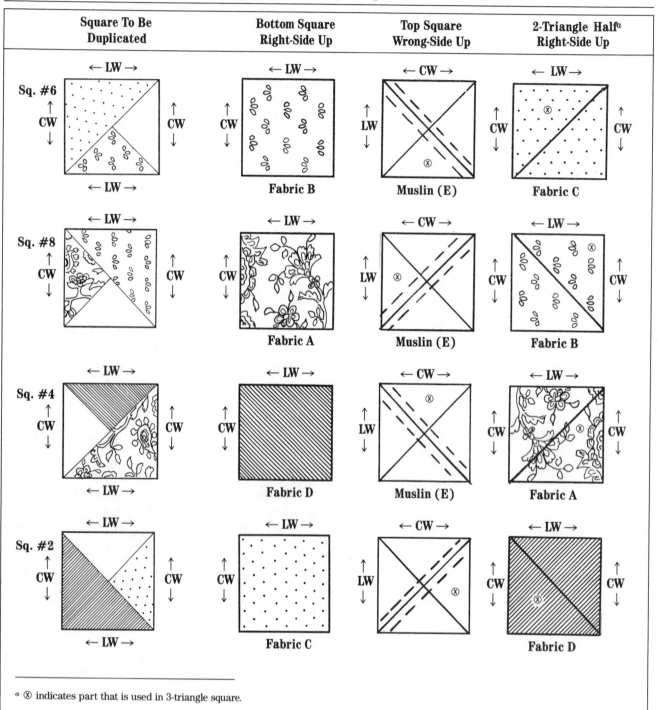

| Square To Be Duplicated | Bottom Square Right-Side Up | Top Square Wrong-Side Up | 2-Triangle Half[a] Right-Side Up |
|---|---|---|---|
| Sq. #6 | Fabric B | Muslin (E) | Fabric C |
| Sq. #8 | Fabric A | Muslin (E) | Fabric B |
| Sq. #4 | Fabric D | Muslin (E) | Fabric A |
| Sq. #2 | Fabric C | Muslin (E) | Fabric D |

[a] ⊗ indicates part that is used in 3-triangle square.

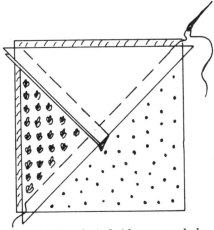

*32. A pieced triangle is laid over a whole-cloth triangle to make a 3-triangle square.*

# Building the Blocks, One Square at a Time

Our next task is to complete an assembly of squares that provides a continuity of design lines, angles that are sharp and clean, and a smooth top surface for quilting, all desirable characteristics of workmanship. We discussed this for whole-cloth squares in "Laying Out and Stitching Up the Squares." Here we will go into more detail and cover pieced squares as well.

Since layout and assembly draws from all of the steps that precede, it is one of the most exciting tasks within the overall process of sew-easy patchworking. It actually serves as a means of measuring the quality of the squares with which you will build your block designs.

It is *here* that you will discover the whys (and just maybe the why-nots) of some of the critical details given to you in chapters preceding—details within topics like fabric construction and choice, grainline direction, maintenance of consistency in grainline within the tasks of measuring, marking, cutting, stitching, piecing, finger-pressing, etc.

I will make a special effort to reference these details as we move through the entire process of block building. One reminder: you are building learning blocks, so mistakes (a few!) *are* allowed. Besides, each "building" experience means you'll do better next time.

## Layout of Squares

The first step is to lay out the squares, right side up, for the design you have chosen to do. Arrange the

squares to duplicate the completed design as illustrated in the Look and See forms in Chapter 4 and in the layout and assembly diagram (p. 112) developed for this purpose. Pages for the Look and See forms are listed here for your convenience:

Nine Patch (p. 56).
Hourglass (p. 61).
Susannah (p. 66).
Ohio Star (p. 71).
Louisiana (p. 76).
Card Tricks (p. 81).

- Four of the above-listed designs have nine squares. Louisiana and Susannah have sixteen squares. The process of layout, as explained herein, applies to every design regardless of the number of squares.

- Make certain that each individual square is placed so that its crosswise grain is on the top as you face the layout. Thus all of the vertical seams to make a row across (those joining squares together) will be on the lengthwise grain, that is, will run up and down. The horizontal seams (those that join the rows together) will be on the crosswise grain, which will run across the design. (The crosswise direction was x'ed on the wrong side of all squares as they were marked earlier.) The crosswise grain will stretch; the lengthwise grain will not; therefore, like grainline edges react in the same way. So it is that the fitting together of squares and rows is more easily accomplished without excessive stretching or easing of fabric as the seams are stitched. The discussion of fabric construction in Chapter 3 will help you better understand the importance of consistency of grainline throughout the total process of patchworking. This is a good time to read it again.

- Even though easier stitching is an important factor in design construction, the obvious effectiveness of a matched fabric pattern in a "directional print" means you will need to turn your attention to this characteristic also. See the color photographs of the learning blocks that have used a directional special print for reference (Nine Patch, Susannah, and Card Tricks).

- The maintenance of grainline consistency is sew easy if all of the previous suggestions for cutting, marking, piecing were followed carefully. See the detailed diagram (Figure 33) for layout and sequence of stitching, and note the following.

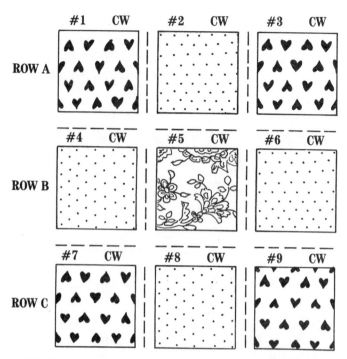

*33. Joining squares to form a block. First, rows are made. Then rows are joined to form a square as in the charts.*

**1.** The squares are numbered at the corner.

**2.** The crosswise grain (CW) is placed at the top as viewed from the right side of each square.

**3.** The squares to be joined together to form a row are indicated with a vertical stitching line between them.

**4.** The rows to be stitched together to form a block are indicated with a horizontal stitching line between them as indicated (— — — —).

**5.** The design as illustrated in Figure 33 is the Nine Patch. The assembly procedure for all sew-easy blocks is alike, despite any differences in patch forms or number of squares.

## Sewing Details

As is the case of every how-to task, there are some matters of housekeeping that must be carefully reviewed before you go forward with the next activity.

• Use the smallest needle that you can comfortably work with. Both sharps and betweens are acceptable for piecing. Reread the supplies list in Chapter 3.

• A short length of thread is easier to work with— 12″ to 18″. If the thread continually snarls or tangles, pull the shorter end out and make it the longer of the two ends coming through the eye of the needle.

• Secure the stitches with one or two short backstitches at both the beginning and ending of every seam. Tug gently on the thread to make sure that it doesn't slip.

• Leave short tails of thread (at least an inch) to avoid any slipping of stitches.

• Do not catch any of the seam allowances of previously joined intersecting seamlines (Fig. 16). These must be left to turn freely to accommodate the directional turning of seams in fingerpressing. Any excess bulk is always apparent as you look at the finished design from the upper side.

• Reread the assembly instructions given earlier in Step 12 (page 92). As presented there, the suggestions applied to the Nine-Patch, the only learning block that has no pieced squares. But once you have pieced the squares to construct an additional learning block, the instructions for assembling the Nine-Patch apply to the joining of squares into rows, and rows into blocks, regardless of the patch forms involved (whole-cloth or pieced), and regardless of the number of squares in the block (9 or 16).

• The stitching of squares into rows is less demanding than is the stitching of rows into blocks, because you have many more seam allowances to deal with when you join rows together. The crosswise seams joining rows together may be stitched together in one of two different ways. The first method utilizes one continuous seam, which begins at the outside edge to your right and ends at the outside edge to your left. Small backstitches are used to secure the seams at both their beginning and ending points, and also at the right and left side of seam allowances involved in the seamline intersections.

• Place these backstitches as close to the vertical seams as is possible without catching the seam allowance. After the first backstitches are made (at the approach side of the intersecting seams), push the needle carefully through the involved seam allowances, close to the vertical seam. Backstitch again as the needle exits to the left of all these seam allowances (see Fig. 35).

- The margin of error created through the use of a continuous seam across the width of the rows is greatly increased: The precise matching of seamlines is difficult to maintain if the pin holding them in place is removed to accommodate the directional turning of the seam allowances during the stitching process. As a result, the fabric has a tendency to shift ahead of your stitching. If the manipulation of the needle through the seam allowances pierces the upper side of the design, the stitch will show; if the backstitches are too far apart at the entry and exit points, they will likely create a hole in the stitching line that is not only obvious, but will weaken the intersection at some future time—during quilting for sure! For this reason, the second method of joining rows is offered below.

- The second method of joining the rows involves the stitching of three or four complete seams, depending on how many squares there are in each row you are joining. Each seam runs across the width of the individual square. Backstitches are used to secure the seam as it begins and ends. Each seam will begin and end at an intersection of seams joining the squares into rows. This gives you an opportunity to begin two of the seams at a matched and stitched intersection (Fig. 36). The first seam is an exception, but the intersection can be checked and repinned behind the intersection while the row seam is backstitched. The location of the backstitches as they relate to the intersections as described for the continuous seam remains the same. This method eliminates the necessity of passing the needle through the seam allowances and increases, I feel, the likelihood of precisely matched seamlines.

- Both methods are illustrated here. Please study the figures in conjunction with the respective descriptions. Both methods require that the row seams be pinned together at matched intersections and outside corners, prior to stitching (see Fig. 34).

## Finger-Pressing

- Finger-pressing, both prior to and during assembly, also contributes to the ease with which we can stitch patches into squares and rows into blocks (and in so doing, it influences the ultimate quality of a block design). Finger-pressing provides a way to equalize the distribution of fabric

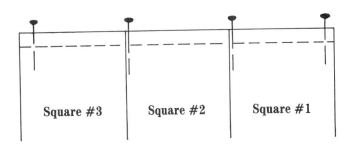

*34. Pinning of rows prior to stitching. You are looking at the reverse side, therefore the sequence of numbering must be reversed also. The seam allowances have been omitted to show the pinning more clearly. If there is any fullness between the pins, the edges can be gently stretched or eased to fit smoothly together as you sew.*

*35. Stitching detail for the backstitch and manipulation of the needle through the seam allowances in the first method for stitching row seams as a continuous seam.*

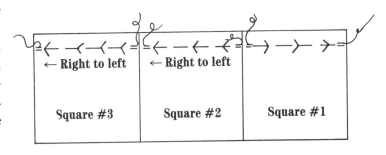

*36. Joining two rows by the second method. (The squares are numbered in reverse order since the row is viewed from the reverse side.) Stitch #2 first, #3 second; then flip the unit over from end to end and stitch #1 square last. The stitching will be done from the intersecting seam toward the outside edge in a right-to-left direction again. Each seam is backstitched as indicated.*

thicknesses at points of intersection, thereby creating a smoother, flatter top surface for quilting at some later time. This begins with the seamlines within a pieced square that may appear in a block design. They must be finger-pressed (or re-pressed!) *before* the squares are stitched together to form the block design. Finger-pressing is a gentle smoothing or creasing of the seamlines between the index finger and the thumb of the left hand, while the right hand is used to guide and support the squares involved. (If you are left-handed, this procedure is reversed.) This smoothing motion must always follow the straight grain of the patches and/or squares involved in the seams being pressed, if you are to avoid distorting them.

- Lay the seamline to be pressed vertically on your left index finger. It will serve as a kind of work surface or ironing board, as it were! Beginning at the edge *away* from you, move your right thumb along the seamline and follow the straight grain, smoothing the fabric away from the seam so as to expose it sharply. This movement of fabric will also be in the same direction as that of the seam allowance underneath.

- Crease the edge of the seam surface that turns away with your thumbnail, but without any vertical stress on the seam itself. Do remember that the seams *inside* all pieced squares are bias and stretch easily. Be very gentle as you press or re-press them prior to stitching.

## Directional Turns of Seams

As a seamline is pressed, the directional turn for that seam is also established. Though the decision as to seam turn is arbitrary, it is essential that you remember that the choice of direction is made to equalize the distribution of fabric thicknesses at the points of intersection. At best, this is sometimes a matter of trial and error, since the turn for one seam must mesh or dovetail with others that intersect it. One of the learning blocks has eight seams that come together in the center of the design—sixteen thicknesses of fabric that you must deal with in stitching! That is why Louisiana is your fifth design for doing! But experience is the best teacher—hence you do learning blocks! We have included photos of the backs of the learning blocks to illustrate (Figs. 37–42) the turns I chose for the six learning blocks. The sequence of numbering the

squares is therefore reversed also because we are looking at their backs—they are read from right to left! (See the Look and See forms in Chapter 3 for reference to the numbering.) Because you will need to refer to these as they relate to the seams within the pieced squares prior to stitching, I have elected to discuss the details of directional turn for five of the blocks that have special needs. These individualized comments will come into play after the stitching process begins. In the meantime, you will find them helpful for the pressing of seams in the pieced squares.

**Nine Patch:** Each of the seamline intersections in the Nine-Patch involves only four thicknesses of fabric. In this case, the seam allowances are simply turned in opposing directions as rows are stitched together to form the entire block design. This task is simplified, however, if the seams joining squares together are pressed first. The seams in the rows can then be matched with greater ease and the stitching process becomes a joy. This building experience will serve you well as you progress through the sequence of learning blocks (see Fig. 37).

**Hourglass:** Hourglass has three pieced squares—two 2-triangle squares and one 4-square square—which is the reason for its inclusion in this discussion. Check the directional turns within these squares against those in Figure 38. If necessary, press or repress the seams therein. Be gentle with the bias seams in the 2-triangle squares!

- The diagonal seams may be turned toward either fabric. Neither choice adds additional fabric thickness to the joining seams of the squares that form Rows A and C (top and bottom rows).

- The intersecting seams in the small squares forming the center square (Square #5) are similar to those of the Nine Patch, in that the center square has two intersecting seams that are also turned in opposing directions. Note that the seams fall in the center of the large square. Thus, they will not affect the joining of the three squares in row B (the center row).

- Before stitching the rows once the pieced squares are finger-pressed (or re-pressed) the design is again arranged, as suggested earlier. This recheck of design arrangement applies to the assembly process for all sew-easy designs. In an effort to avoid repetitious instruction, I will not say this again. Just remember that it is a *necessary part of every design assembly.*

*37.  Back of Nine-Patch block, showing turning of seam allowances.*

- In order to avoid any "show-through" of dark color in the off-white squares (#2, 4, 6, and 8 in Hourglass) the vertical seams joining the squares into rows were turned toward the darker color (see Fig. 38).
- Once *these* turns were determined, the two crosswise seams joining the rows together were stitched. The four intersecting points carry only four thicknesses of fabric; therefore, the two row seams could turn either *up or down.*
- Look now at the illustration for this design (Fig. 38). Please note that *both* row seams in Hourglass were turned *away* from the center of the design. Why? I have *two* dark seamlines in the #5 square

*38. Back of Hourglass block, showing turning of seam allowances.*

turning into off-white squares. But look with me at the alternatives!

- Had I turned both crosswise seams up or both down, I would now have *three* dark seamlines in off-white squares. Had I turned both crosswise row seams *toward the center*, I would have *four* dark seamlines in off-white squares!

- I say all of this to tell you that the turning direction established by finger-pressing is a matter of *personal judgment*. There *are* no rules! *If* the thicknesses of fabric are distributed equally, other factors affecting the "look" of a given design will, in all likelihood, involve the necessity of a tradeoff. *You* will determine what these will be for any

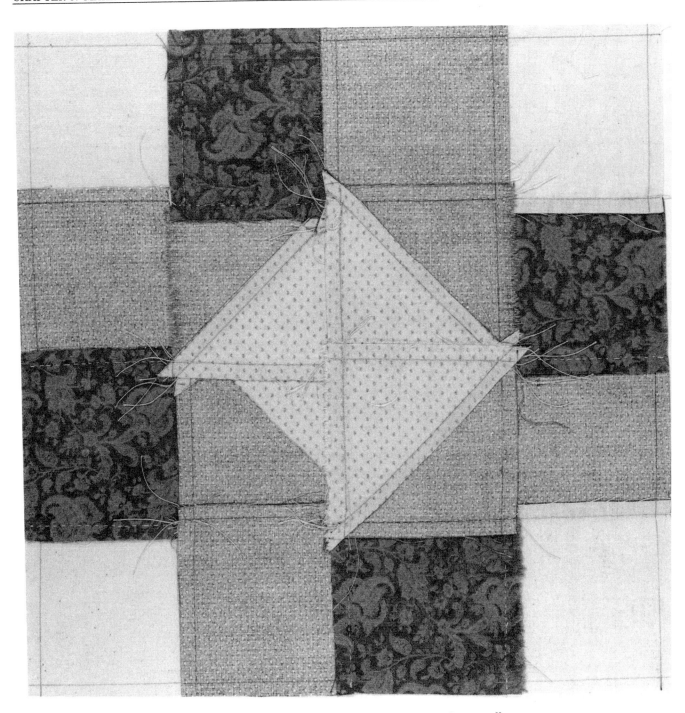

*39. Back of Susannah, showing directional turning of seam allowances.*

given design. Remember that the turns as illustrated herein represent *my* judgment. They are offered as suggestions. I hope they will be helpful.

**Susannah:** Susannah has 4 pieced squares. See Figure 39 for the directional turns of the seam allowances. Be gentle with the bias seams in the 2-triangle squares when you press the seams before joining.

**Ohio Star:** This design presents some special requirements for directional turning of seams so as to create an equitable distribution of fabric in both of the crosswise seams that join the rows together. This is the first design we have done to carry four pieced squares, all of which are 4-triangle squares.

• Ohio Star also involves the intersection of six seams at four different points. Look at the illustra-

*40. Back of Ohio Star block, showing directional turning of seam allowances.*

tion depicting these joinings (Fig. 40). They fall at the four corners of the center square (Square #5).

- The *vertical seams* joining the three squares in each of the three rows almost turn themselves into the adjacent whole-cloth squares. This turn

thereby meshes with the turn seamline as the row seam is stitched.

- But there is still the matter of the diagonal seam-lines within the pieced squares that must be dealt with. They are, as you can see, simply turned away

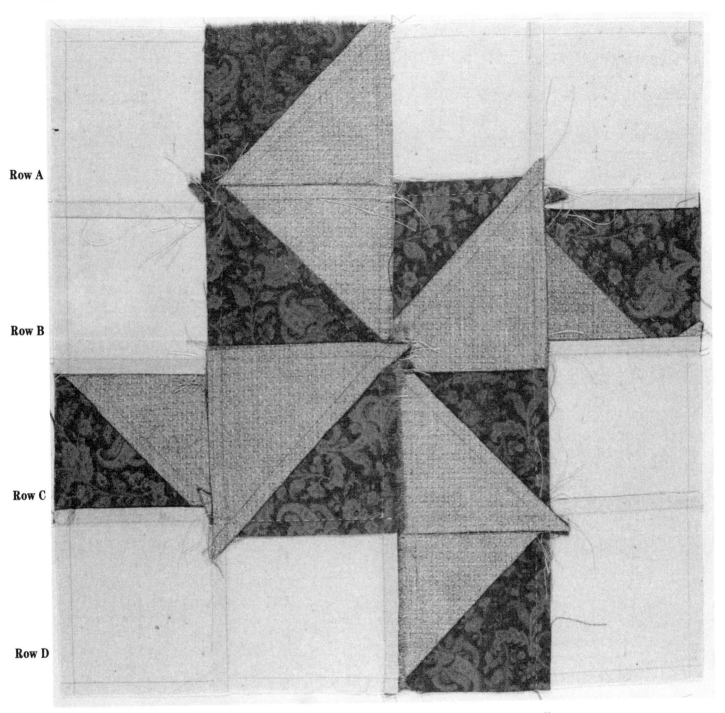

Row A

Row B

Row C

Row D

*41. Back of Louisiana block, showing directional turning of seam allowances.*

from the vertical seam. This therefore, forms sharp angles, which serve as the points of the star, and this makes the stitching of the rows much easier. Both row seams are treated in like manner so as to provide a top surface that is smooth and flat.

**Louisiana:** This design at first glance presents a confusing jumble of seamlines and tails of thread (Fig. 41). The confusion lessens, however, if you concentrate on the individual squares within each individual row. The turns, as illustrated, will be easy to duplicate in your learning block.

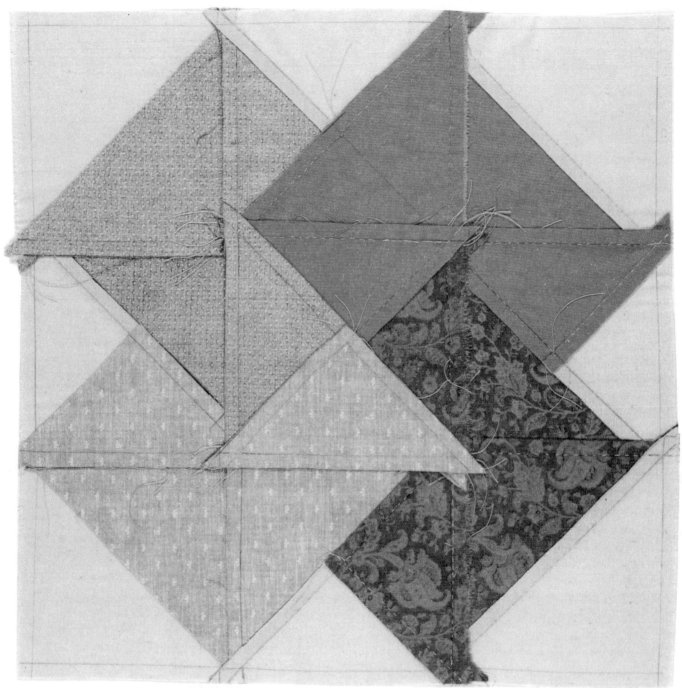

*42. Back of Card Tricks block, showing directional turning of seam allowances.*

- With the turns in the pieced squares out of the way, you are ready to join rows together. Rows A + B and C + D are alike in make-up and will be treated in like manner as they are stitched together.

- The seams which join rows B and C present a different kind of seamline. It is here you must deal with the intersection of eight seams and/or six-

teen thicknesses of fabric. This intersection falls in the center of the block design and becomes the focal point when viewed from the upper side. The effectiveness of the Windmill that is thereby formed is dependent, in large measure, on the precision with which the intersecting seams are matched and pinned prior to stitching, so the establishment of directional turn of seamlines in conjunction with finger-pressing does have some important implications for successful outcomes for your patchworking efforts.

**Card Tricks:** This design, the last of six learning blocks, obviously offers the greatest challenge to our skills in sew-easy patchworking. Card Tricks pulls together all of the previous requirements for skill in both aspects of beautiful—aesthetics and workmanship. The design contains nine pieced squares. Needless to say, there are numerous seams that must be brought together in such a way as to equalize the distribution of fabric thicknesses and, in so doing, enhance the total effect of the four chevrons that fit together in a seemingly impossible way when viewed from the upper side of the finished design.

- As usual, the squares within each individual row become the starting point. The turning directions of patches within each square can be duplicated with ease as you view the illustration provided here (Figure 42). The turning direction for the vertical seams that join the squares into individual rows is also apparent and can be duplicated with little difficulty.

- This brings us up to the task of joining rows together to form the total design. If the directional turns suggested for the diagonal seams in the pieced squares were finger-pressed before the squares were joined together to form three rows and if the suggested turns for the vertical seamlines were also finger-pressed after joining the squares into rows, the rows are now ready to be stitched together to form the total design as illustrated in both black and white and color.

## Review of Assembly Steps

It is always in order to suggest that you check the tasks just preceding before beginning another. Mistakes are better dealt with as you make them!

- Arrange the squares to duplicate the design you are doing. See the swatched paste-up for each learning block and the charted diagrams for layout and assembly.

- Finger-press (or re-press) the seams in any pieced square within the design you are doing.

- Stitch the squares together to form rows.

- Finger-press the vertical seams joining the squares together.

- Check the arrangement of squares within the rows against the original layout.

- Stitch rows A, B, and C (and D, if there is one) together to form the total block design.

- Finger-press the two seam allowances for the rows together in one direction.

- Check your progress against the above listing of activities. Make sure that none of them are overlooked.

- Check your workmanship skills as reflected on the top side of the design. Did you achieve the desired characteristics of *beautiful*?

# Borders: Frame-Ups Are Nice

Borders and quilting are two optional additions to the process of "piecing" patchwork; they are offered to provide you with the opportunity to use your trial blocks as single patchwork pillows or as framed pictures. The instructions presented here do not apply to the setting together of multiple squares for a larger quilt face for bed, wall, or sofa. The details of this particular process (setting a quilt top) is better dealt with in a separate sew-easy doing.

We can provide emphasis to the designs we pieced through the use of borders or sashing. Like a painting, a quilt design is usually seen to better advantage when "framed" by a border. Our task will be to attach a border to a block so that it is square both before and after the attachment. To make borders for your learning block:

- Choose fabric of a color that sets off your block well. Place your block on several background colors at the fabric store or in your home supply of fabrics, to get an idea of how the borders will harmonize with your block, before you make a choice. You will need about ¼ yard of fabric to make the borders for a 12½″ × 12½″ block.

- Wash, dry and iron the fabric.

- Cut or tear border strips of 2¾″ width on the crosswise grain of the fabric. You will need border strips of the following sizes (these include an extra ½″ in the length for trimming later on):

  A  2¾″ × 13″        C  2¾″ × 15¼″
  B  2¾″ × 15¼″      D  2¾″ × 16½″

The letters refer to the borders labels in Figure 43.

- Press the border strips carefully after you have cut or torn them to size. Stretch them slightly to eliminate the rippling of the torn edge if you have torn them.

- Pin and baste the border strips to the pieced block in a clockwise direction, as illustrated in Figure 43, with right sides of the pieced block and the border strip fabric facing.

- Using the same stitch as used for piecing the blocks, stitch the borders to the block, with ¼″ seam allowances. Work with the block side up; seam allowances were marked on it earlier, re-member? If not, carefully mark them now. Begin with border A as shown in Figure 43 and work in a clockwise direction, adding B, C and then D. Re-member to avoid stitching down the seam al-lowances of the block's pieced squares when at-taching the borders. Leave them free by passing a needle under the previously made seam allowance when you come to it, as you did when you joined the rows earlier (see Fig. 35).

- As you attach each border, cut away the extra length of the border that extends beyond the square. Pull a thread in the border so that its track will act as a cutting guide. This provides a perfect right-angle joining, which means a square square! Note that we are not using mitred corners; mitred corners for borders are weaker than butt-joined seams. Mitres also present problems when cov-ered cords are used as an edge finish for pillows.

- Backstitch on both sides of all crossed seams. You have two or three!

- Press the block and border seams towards the border.

## Quilting by Design, Without Hoops or Frames

Next we'll quilt the square block to which we just added the borders. Our task is to do this in such a fashion that the block remains square, even after quilting. We'll use small, invisible stitches that are uniform in length (about 5 to 12 stitches to the inch is desirable; beginners usually take larger stitches, so don't be discouraged if yours are larger at first). Use a "between" sized needle (size 5 to 10) and 100% cotton hand quilting thread, if possible. All-purpose thread may be used if necessary. Choose a color of thread that is as close as possible to the color of the patch you're going to quilt; change colors as neces-

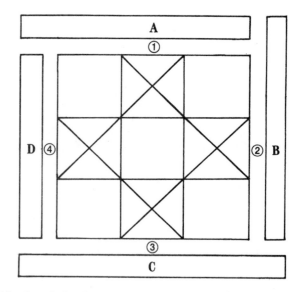

43. Attach borders in a clockwise direction, starting with A.

sary, based on your design. A thimble to push the needle through is also very helpful.

You'll also need a whole cloth square of backing fabric that is 14″ × 14″, 2″ larger in each dimension than the block. In addition, get a square of 100% bonded polyester batting of the same size as the backing. This provides the loft in the quilt.

At this point, you are ready to stack the quilting "sandwich" together in this order:

- Backing: wrong side up! I usually tape the backing over the grid of my cutting board to hold it square (and taut) for the pinning, basting and quilting process.

- Batting

- Finished block: right side up.

You can quilt your block without hoops or frames, if you carefully do three things: pin the sandwich together directionally (see Fig. 44), baste it together directionally, and quilt it together directionally. The quilting is done in the seamlines of each shape so that it stands out in relief. The quilting stitch is a simple running that is short, small and uniform. It's sew easy! The order of doing the three procedures is shown in Figure 44. Please note that you are work-ing from the center out, smoothing away any excess fabric ahead of the pins as you go. This is necessary to preserve the squareness of your square.

Thread a "between" with an 18″ length of quilting thread, and make a single knot in one end. Starting from the top, sew through the batting on a seamline

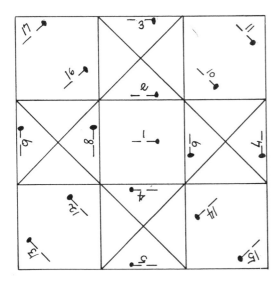

44. *Order for directional pinning, basting, and quilting of single trial blocks for patchwork pillows or framed pictures. The block is quilted along the seamlines, starting from the center and working out.*

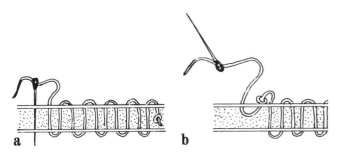

45. *a: To begin, tie a knot and pull it through to the batting to hide it. b: To end the thread, tie a single knot and pull it through to the batting before cutting the thread.*

you want to stitch and come up again about 1″ away. Pull the knot gently through, pushing it with your finger if necessary, to bury the knot in the batting. Take a backstitch to anchor the knot in place, and proceed with stitching, going through all three layers with each stitch (see Fig. 45). To end a thread, tie a knot, stitch into and out of the batting and top layer, and pull the knot through into the batting. Trim off the excess thread.

## Evaluating Your Patchwork

Now it's time to measure the quality of your patchwork against established standards of good design, which includes both workmanship skills and aes-

thetics. First, let's measure your accomplishments as they relate to the aesthetics of design.

- Do the colors/patterns work together to provide the qualities of beautiful as defined in Chapter 2?
- Do you experience a feeling of balance in the distribution of color and pattern, or do you have too many of the heavy colors, more visible colors in the same area of the total design?
- Do you have at least one center of interest? If you have two, is one of them more important than the other?
- Are the colors and patterns properly scaled as they relate to both the existence of other patterns and as to the sizes of the patches in which they appear? If you have more than one pattern, do they share a color or colors in common?
- When you look at your finished design, do you see a jumble of confusion between shapes, colors, patterns, or do you see the entire block as a pleasing whole?
- If your answers to any of the above showed you weren't totally successful, which of the qualities did you fail to establish to your satisfaction?

Now let's think about your workmanship skills:

- Do the patches and/or squares fit together?
- Are all of the design lines continuous? Do the seams meet where colors and shapes change?
- Did you lose any of the sharp angles to seamlines that clipped them away?
- Are the seamlines smooth and flat, without lumps or bumps on the upper surface?
- Does your finished block twist or wrinkle? Does it lie smooth and flat?
- Are the squares all cut on the straight of grain?
- If you have used a directional fabric, is the grainline direction consistently used within all the patches in which it appears?

Did you measure up against both standards—those that relate to the aesthetics of design and those that relate to good workmanship? If so, you should be very proud of yourself. If not, don't despair. Go back and reread the introductory material and try to figure out where you went wrong. As you practice cutting and stitching, your workmanship is likely to improve. Studying successful color harmonies (in flowers, paintings, or fabrics) may also help if you are having aesthetic problems.

<h1 style="text-align:center">—6—</h1>

# Additional Heirloom Designs

## Introduction

Now it's *your* turn to choose designs for doing, without *any* concern for their provision of a learning experience for a particular patchworking skill. Because you have already gained the necessary know-how for these through your construction of the learning blocks, the heirloom patterns given in this chapter allow you to choose based solely on the personal appeal of the design itself. You are thereby free to exercise your own sense of creativity as you work (and play) with the two most exciting ingredients of patchworking—color and pattern. But just in case you should need an occasional nudge to move you in a forward direction (and with greater confidence), I offer the following visual clues:

- A color reproduction of each of the 18 completed heirloom designs, given in the color section of this book. These are models showing my color and pattern choices—you will probably want to choose your own.

- A reduced-size swatched paste-up clearly depicting the component squares and patches that form each design, based on the full-color model. This "trial" block provides a quick and easy way to evaluate your selection *and* distribution of color and pattern before the design is actually constructed. You can use it with your own fabrics, as described in Chapter 3.

- A *block analysis* that tells you all the things you need to know before you *do* anything. This gives you a beforehand study of the factors that you must deal with during construction.

- A completed planning form, Tie It All Together, which tells you how many whole-cloth squares you need to cut, how big they must be, and the fabric from which they must be cut to create the heirloom block. This also is based on my color model; substitute your own fabrics in this after you choose them.

This chapter includes an additional visual tool for doing—a how-to review of the illustrated use of color/pattern for six heirloom designs, which I selected as representative examples of components within every block design in the section. These reviews are offered as a learning support for your move into the building of eighteen beautiful heirlooms of your very own. Each of the reviewed designs is shown in the color section.

As you create your heirloom blocks, remember that you can refer to learnings covered earlier in the choosing chapter (Chapter 3) and in the learning blocks chapter if you need to review a particular procedure. See the contents and index of this book for guidance. For example, if you need to review marking 2-triangle squares for your heirloom block, turn to the pages in Chapter 5 that describe cutting 2-triangle squares.

# Analysis of Color and Pattern Selection in Six Heirloom Blocks

## Attic Windows (see color page D and Fig. 46)

### Special Characteristics

A well-defined color plan, beautifully executed to form fascinating illusions of depth within multiples of a single pieced square.

### Contributions to the Qualities of "Beautiful"

**Balance:** If we measure the weight of the small black squares against that of the combined area of rose and pink, we not only see but also feel (and enjoy) the intangible quality of visual balance created by perceptions of color.

**Emphasis:** When the collective contributions of contrast and variety (difference and opposition), within all the various elements of this block design—size, shape, pattern, color value and intensity—are put together, the windows are formed. They become the focus of the design. Thus the quality of *emphasis* is provided for our viewing pleasure.

The "telling" of a process is important, but showing *and* telling is far more effective! Look at the details of the window—or rather, the illusion of the window. How does one create something that comes and goes (or seems to)? This effect has to do with our visual perception of color—how we see it. The Color Perception Chart in Chapter 3 was developed for this purpose.

When you look at the visual details of the window, the black square (the window opening) appears to recede, to move farther away, deeper into the "walls" around it. On the other hand, the warm, softly shaded pink and rose "walls" seem to advance or move toward you. They grow in size. Thus they create an interesting illusion of depth.

I call your attention to three specific not-so-little contributors of emphasis—first, the combined use of three different patterns. Using so many patterns is permissible *if* they differ in scale and share a common color. They do! And beautifully!

Now look at the arrangement of the grainline direction in the rose-colored patches. Although this requires some attention to detail during construc-

tion, it pays tremendous dividends in viewer satisfaction once the design is completed. The how-to of handling directional fabrics was discussed when we did the Card Tricks learning block in Chapter 5. The techniques are sew easy.

I have referred to the "small black squares" in Attic Windows already, but in terms of visual weight. Think about them now in terms of pattern. The fan speaks of femininity in both color and motif. It also underscores the importance of patterned fabric as a reliable planning source for the choosing of color. The pink in the patterned fan material is repeated in the other patterned fabrics.

**Scale/Proportion:** Look at the variations in pattern scale as it relates to the space in which it appears, and look at the unequal division of color, which contributes to the quality of proportion that is hereby established.

**Rhythm:** The visibility of the black square provides an organized movement of viewer interest throughout the entire design area. This smoothness of view is also a pleasurable experience.

**Unity:** This last quality is vital because it exists to the degree that the preceding qualities exist. The visible "togetherness" or oneness of all the elements—color, pattern, shapes, spaces, whether large/small, dull/bright, dark or light—*do* work together to create this quality. Necessary? Indeed! And exciting, even fun to do.

### Comments

Because the how-to's for the creation of the design qualities as presented in Attic Windows are applicable to all other designs, this discussion will serve as a doing tool for all your patchworking efforts. Use it!

## Battlegrounds (see color page F and Fig. 47)

### Special Characteristics

The Battlegrounds model has an absence of monotony or busyness despite the repetitious use of size, shape, color, pattern and patch form—the tools with which we create, in a very small space, the qualities of all things beautiful.

### Contributions to the Qualities of "Beautiful"

A design made by using one patch form over and over is sometimes referred to as a one-patch quilt, a memory quilt, or more often, a scrap quilt when it is used in a larger area. It reflects a long-held attitude of "waste not—want not," which even today is typical of patchworkers everywhere.

The repetitious use of triangles (32 of them) necessitates a kind of trial-and-error doing of the design for evaluation before construction. A swatched paste-up provides a quick and easy way to do this.

The sameness in this design also emphasizes the need for a color plan that accommodates the prescribed functions of background, foreground, and accent areas as defined in the Procedural Outline for Choosing Colors and Patterns in Chapter 3. We need a color plan that will increase or decrease the visual size of the triangles as necessary, will call attention to (or create) an interest area within the total block design, and finally, one that will tie all the little triangles together to provide the qualities of beautiful! Why don't we look at the way I attempted to do this (see color page F).

**Balance:** According to the Color Perceptions Chart in Chapter 3, the visibility, weight, and size of the darker, warmer variations of colors are visually *increased*, while these same dimensions in the lighter, cooler colors are visually *decreased*. Therefore, the small area of dark brown and rust is balanced by a larger area of light browns and beige. Once again, the quality of balance, which we can see and feel (and enjoy) is established.

**Emphasis:** As I view the completed design in color, I see a single neutral non-color, but in interesting variations that move from the dark, deep shades of a cool brown, through the warmth of rust, the brightness of terra cotta, the soft dullness of camel, and finally to the quietness of a warm, restful value of beige. Because it is also a noncompetitive color, beige provides a perfect background or "nesting" place for the highly visible triangles of colors as just named.

When these triangles of color are combined with those which in contrast are almost devoid of color, it is the shapes themselves, the triangles per se, that become the real focus of the design. As a result, the sameness of the various elements becomes an asset rather than a liability. There *is* no monotony of pattern, color, or shape. Thus the quality of emphasis is established again, for our viewing pleasure.

**Scale/Proportion:** The number of triangles in the background area versus that of the combined

areas of foreground and accent are equal, therefore poorly proportioned. However, because color *is* as we see it, we perceive the dark browns, warm rusts, and bright terra cotta in the foreground/accent areas as larger, heavier, and more visible than are the lighter value of the beige in the background.

Thus, the division of colors is visually unequal—a division necessary to the creation of pleasing proportions. Please note that the variety of scale and density of pattern in each one of the sixteen colored triangles is a part of the visual interest of this design. Look, too, at the scale of the various patterns as it relates to the small triangles in which they appear.

**Rhythm:** This quality by definition offers "a smooth flow of visual interest that moves the viewer from one element to another in an organized fashion." The "elements" here are color and pattern; they are used in like spaces—sixteen small triangles.

Look at the logistics of this challenging task: We have sixteen triangles, eight different colors and patterns, four rows of colored and patterned triangles, and all of these within an area of just twelve inches! *This* means that every patterned triangle must be used twice. And this means (if we eliminate the aspect of confusion) the respective triangles must be placed in every other row of patch forms.

Despite the fact that two triangles in the same color and pattern appear entirely too close to each other (you can surely find them), the quality of rhythm *is* at work for your viewing pleasure.

**Unity:** Since the presence of the other four qualities has already been justified, it suffices to say here that the thirty-two little triangles in this design no longer stand alone. They *do* become a part of a whole, and additionally the completed design is truly beautiful.

## Clay's Choice (see color page G and Fig. 48)

### Special Characteristics

Four thin parallelograms (diamonds) are formed by the unusual joining of eight right-angle triangles to create this longtime favorite motif—the windmill. Here it is a little unusual in that the shape and color arrangement provides a feeling of grace and femininity. In addition to this, I want to call your attention to the near-perfect on-grain piecing and cutting of the shapes in which the apricot geometric print appears.

## Contributions to the Qualities of "Beautiful"

**Balance:** As usual, the space within this design includes the background area (in a soft warm beige), the foreground area (in varying shades of olive, coral, and apricot), and the accent area (the apricot geometric print). The combined areas of background and accent provide the visual balance that is needed when measured against the heavy visibility of the olive print.

**Emphasis:** The dominant fabric—the olive print—is used to emphasize the windmill as the center of viewing interest within the total design. The repetitious use of the soft apricot serves as a supporting element. The near concealment of seamlines between the adjoining triangles that form the arms of the windmill is a plus for emphasis of the windmill arms. Note the variations of both scale and color in the prints, which account for the almost invisible seamlines.

**Scale/Proportion:** The two patterns appearing in this particular design *do* differ in scale; they also share a common color—both are prerequisites to the mixing of patterns. Take note of the accuracy of piecing as seen in the on-grain edges of the shapes in which the olive print appears. Occasionally it is not possible to match designs in crosswise and lengthwise edges of fabric. If the combination of the two edges is too objectionable, the fabric should be avoided for quilting.

**Rhythm:** The soft blending of color values takes you into the convergence of the windmill arms, out to the edges of the total area of the design to the corners, back into the center and out again—very pleasant!

**Unity:** The complete lack of clutter within this particular design creates a feeling of oneness that is soothing and restful. I predict that this design will become one of the favorite patterns for the just right little girl in your family. I believe that it has much to say about the many functions of color and pattern.

## Clown's Choice (see color page F and Fig. 49)

### Special Characteristics

The softly blended colors of an all-over miniprint (very old-fashioned) and consistency of grainline direction in the orange paw print used in the five 4-triangle squares combine to create a strong plus for the rightness of selection and distribution of color and pattern, as is reflected by the presence of all of the qualities of good design.

## Contributions to the Qualities of "Beautiful"

**Balance:** The density of the all-over miniprint squares, with color variations in pastel shades of canteloupe, peachy beige, turquoise, and seafoam appears somewhat heavier than do the 4-triangle squares of rich, warm shades of yellow-orange with the directional paw print. The high visibility of triangles is, however, pleasantly balanced by the miniprinted squares.

**Emphasis:** Emphasis is achieved through the unusual interest of the consistent grainline direction, which has been maintained throughout the entire design area. This technique is sew easy and is discussed at length in the section on Card Tricks in Chapter 5.

**Scale/Proportion:** The two fabric patterns used are pleasingly scaled to each other and to the spaces in which they appear. Because the divisions of color and pattern are made unequally, the proportions existing within the total area are pleasing to our view.

**Rhythm:** While it is difficult to say which element catches my attention first, it will suffice to say that the viewing process is one of absolute pleasure! Attention to detail in color arrangement and selection makes an important contribution as well.

**Unity:** Because the previous qualities exist, the quality of togetherness exists also. The old-fashioned charm of this design, combined with the interesting effects of directional design, is outstanding.

## Dutchman's Puzzle (see color page E and Fig. 50)

### Special Characteristics

This too is a long-favored design motif—another windmill—but in this case, one that is heavier in appearance than is the one just seen in Clay's Choice. The blue print windmill arms are formed by a mirror-image joining of two right-angle triangles.

### Contributions to the Qualities of "Beautiful"

All five of the necessary aesthetic qualities—balance, emphasis, scale/proportion, rhythm, and unity—are present. The three colors and patterns were chosen to accommodate the functional demands of the area in which they appear—the background, foreground, and accent areas. For example, the beige background provides a "nesting" place for the entire design. As such, it emphasizes the various elements in the total area. It requires a quiet, non-competitive fabric, neutral in color, or, if patterned, a small scaled one-color print. I have chosen a soft, warm beige that strongly supports the important elements of foreground and accent areas.

The various contrasts in color value and in pattern scale and density combine to make the dark blue-purple/rose/taupe fabric one of dominance. This in turn is placed in the foreground area, making the windmill the major focus of the design. Because the warm, dulled shade of rose is highly visible, it is properly placed in the accent area, where it gives support to the major element, the blue print windmill.

Even though both colors fill equal numbers of large triangles (four), they appear to create *unequal* divisions of color, a proportion that is desirable. Unequal? But how so? The scattered arrangement of the rose triangles creates an illusion of diminished size. The concentration of the dark blue-purple triangles forming the windmill creates an illusion of increased size and weight, thereby producing the unequal division of color/pattern.

Both colors serve to direct our visual interest in an organized fashion, moving us first to the center, then out to the edges of the design, around, and back to the center—the windmill again. This *is* the quality of rhythm.

Hopefully, all of this tells you that the choosing of a pleasing color scheme just isn't enough! You must also find the "just right" space in which to place the ingredients. And this task is truly exciting, creative, and extremely satisfying.

### Evening Star (see color page H and Fig. 51)

#### Special Characteristics

This particular design depicts for me the true sense of a patchwork that was typical in the beginnings of this lovely needle skill. Let me describe it in simple words or phrases that will hopefully take you into the same long ago: Traditional! Impressive! Simple! Soft, dulled color is cool, quiet, restful, "country." The model is a one-color design in an ever-popular motif, one that is diagonally set.

### Contributions to the Qualities of "Beautiful"

**Balance:** Even though the design utilizes only one color, the change from solid color to the minute details of color in the print serves to break up any feelings of monotony. This in itself provides a pleasing sense of visual balance as the design is viewed in its entirety.

**Emphasis:** The change from solid to pattern creates a special emphasis on the star itself as the center of interest within the total area. The diagonal setting, which is somewhat unusual, is another point of emphasis that increases the importance of the star.

**Rhythm:** The division of fabric pattern moves us into the center, out to the edges of the points, around the entire area, back to the center, and out again. This is an organization of movement that is in no way hampered by a lack of contrast in any element.

**Scale/Proportion:** The area of patterned fabric versus that of solid fabric creates an unequal division of fabric surface treatment that is extremely quieting in effect. The scale of the print is certainly appropriate to the size of the patches in which it appears.

**Unity:** Despite the fact that this design appears in only one color, it strongly represents a togetherness of all the elements involved without a trace of monotony.

# Analysis of Heirloom Patterns

On pages 129–147, a swatched paste-up of each of the heirloom designs is given, based on the models shown in the color photo section. To plan a block with a design, copy the appropriate blank Choose a Design chart (either 9 or 16 squares) from the Appendix. Use the chart to make the swatched paste-up of the design you choose, with your own choices of fabrics. The Tie It All Together chart summarizes the amount and size of each fabric you need to cut to make a 12″ × 12″ block. Paste your own fabric swatches in the appropriate places in the Tie It All Together Chart, so you know what size squares to cut to make your block.

## Attic Windows

- 16 Squares
- 20 Patches
- 2 Patch forms
- 4 Pieced squares
- 12 Whole-cloth squares
- 4 Bias seams
- 5 Converging seams
- 10 Thicknesses of fabric

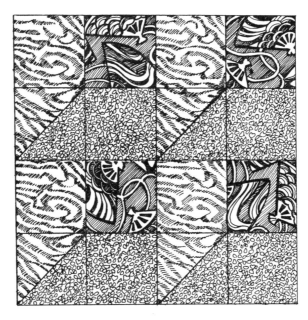

46. *Swatched paste-up for Attic Windows (see also color page D). Use your own fabrics and substitute them in a blank 16-square Choose a Design chart, copied from the one in the Appendix.*

## Tie It All Together: A Summary Chart for Cutting

**Name of block design:** *Attic Windows*

| Which fabrics? | Fabric swatch[a] | How many squares? | How big? | Patch form involved? |
|---|---|---|---|---|
| **A** | | 4 | 3½″ × 3½″ | 1-Patch |
| | | | | |
| | | | | |
| **B** | | 4 | 3½″ × 3½″ | 1-Patch |
| | | 2 | 3⅞″ × 3⅞″ | 2-Triangle |
| | | | | |
| **C** | | 4 | 3½″ × 3½″ | 1-Patch |
| | | 2 | 3⅞″ × 3⅞″ | 2-Triangle |
| | | | | |

[a] Color or paste in the fabric swatches to match your swatched paste-up.

129

## Battlegrounds

- 16 Squares
- 32 Patches
- 1 Patch form
- 16 Pieced squares
- 16 Bias seams
- 6 Converging seams
- 12 Thicknesses of fabric

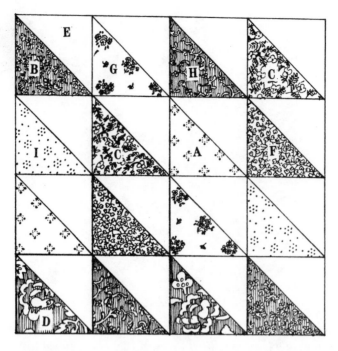

47. *Swatched paste-up for Battlegrounds (see also color page F). Use your own fabrics and substitute them in a blank 16-square Choose a Design chart, copied from the one in the Appendix, to make your own swatched paste-up.*

## Tie It All Together: A Summary Chart for Cutting

**Name of block design:** _Battlegrounds_

| Which fabrics? | Fabric swatch[a] | How many squares? | How big? | Patch form involved? |
|---|---|---|---|---|
| A | | _1_ | _3⅞″ × 3⅞″_ | _2-Triangle_ |
| B | | _1_ | _3⅞″ × 3⅞″_ | _2-Triangle_ |
| C | | _1_ | _3⅞″ × 3⅞″_ | _2-Triangle_ |

[a] Color or paste in the fabric swatches to match your swatched paste-up.

### Tie It All Together, continued

Name of block design: *Battlegrounds*

| Which fabrics? | Fabric swatch[a] | How many squares? | How big? | Patch form involved? |
|---|---|---|---|---|
| D |  | *1* | *3⅞″ × 3⅞″* | *2-Triangle* |
| | | | | |
| | | | | |
| E | (Beige) | *8* | *3⅞″ × 3⅞″* | *2-Triangle* |
| | | | | |
| | | | | |
| F |  | *1* | *3⅞″ × 3⅞″* | *2-Triangle* |
| | | | | |
| | | | | |
| G |  | *1* | *3⅞″ × 3⅞″* | *2-Triangle* |
| | | | | |
| | | | | |
| H |  | *1* | *3⅞″ × 3⅞″* | *2-Triangle* |
| | | | | |
| | | | | |
| I | 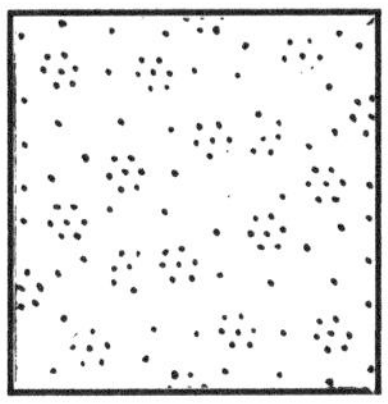 | *1* | *3⅞″ × 3⅞″* | *2-Triangle* |
| | | | | |
| | | | | |

## Clay's Choice

- 16 Squares
- 24 Patches
- 2 Patch forms
- 8 Pieced squares
- 8 Whole-cloth squares
- 8 Bias seams
- 8 Converging seams
- 16 Thicknesses of fabric

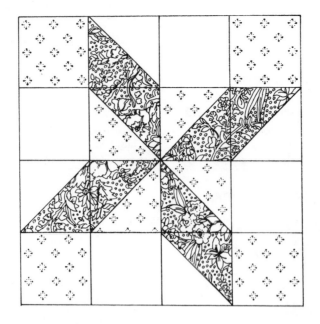

*48. Swatched paste-up for Clay's Choice (see also color page G). Use your own fabrics and substitute them in a blank 16-square Choose a Design chart, copied from the one in the Appendix, to make your own swatched paste-up.*

## Tie It All Together: A Summary Chart for Cutting

**Name of block design:** *Clay's Choice*

| Which fabrics? | Fabric swatch[a] | How many squares? | How big? | Patch form involved? |
|---|---|---|---|---|
| **A** | | *4* | *3½″ × 3½″* | *1-Patch* |
| | | *2* | *3⅞″ × 3⅞″* | *2-Triangle* |
| | | | | |
| **B** | | *4* | *3⅞″ × 3⅞″* | *2-Triangle* |
| | | | | |
| | | | | |
| **C (Muslin)** | | *4* | *3½″ × 3½″* | *1-Patch* |
| | | *2* | *3⅞″ × 3⅞″* | *2-Triangle* |
| | | | | |

[a] Color or paste in the fabric swatches to match your swatched paste-up.

## Clown's Choice

- 9 Squares
- 24 Patches
- 2 Patch forms
- 5 Pieced squares
- 4 Whole-cloth squares
- 10 Bias seams
- 6 Converging seams
- 12 Thicknesses of fabric

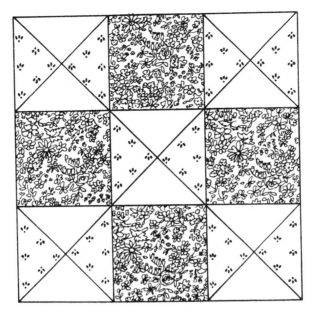

*49. Swatched paste-up for Clown's Choice (see also color page F). Use your own fabrics and substitute them in a blank 16-square Choose a Design chart, copied from the one in the Appendix, to make your own swatched paste-up.*

## Tie It All Together: A Summary Chart for Cutting

**Name of block design:** *Clown's Choice*

| Which fabrics? | Fabric swatch[a] | How many squares? | How big? | Patch form involved? |
|---|---|---|---|---|
| **A** | | 5 | 5⅜″ × 5⅜″ | 4-Triangle |
| | | | | |
| | | | | |
| **B** | | 4 | 4½″ × 4½″ | 1-Patch |
| | | | | |
| | | | | |
| **C** (Light Orange) | | 5 | 5⅜″ × 5⅜″ | 4-Triangle |
| | | | | |
| | | | | |

[a] Color or paste in the fabric swatches as identified in "Look and See."

## Dutchman's Puzzle

- 16 Squares
- 32 Patches
- 1 Patch form
- 16 Pieced squares
- 16 Bias seams
- 8 Converging seams
- 16 Thicknesses of fabric

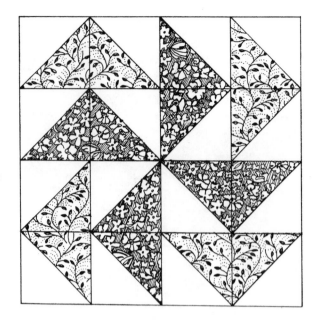

50. *Swatched paste-up for Dutchman's Puzzle (see also color page E). Use your own fabrics and substitute them in a blank 16-square Choose a Design chart, copied from the one in the Appendix, to make your own swatched paste-up.*

## Tie It All Together: A Summary Chart for Cutting

**Name of block design:** _Dutchman's Puzzle_

| Which fabrics? | Fabric swatch[a] | How many squares? | How big? | Patch form involved? |
|---|---|---|---|---|
| A | | 4 | 3⅞" × 3⅞" | 2-Triangle |
| B | | 4 | 3⅞" × 3⅞" | 2-Triangle |
| C (Beige) | | 8 | 3⅞" × 3⅞" | 2-Triangle |

[a] Color or paste in the fabric swatches to match your swatched paste-up.

## Evening Star

- 16 Squares
- 24 Patches
- 2 Patch forms
- 8 Pieced squares
- 8 Whole-cloth squares
- 8 Bias seams
- 6 Converging seams
- 12 Thicknesses of fabric

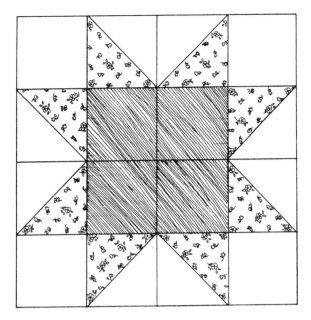

*51. Swatched paste-up for Evening Star (see also color page H). Use your own fabrics and substitute them in a blank 16-square Choose a Design chart, copied from the one in the Appendix, to make your own swatched paste-up.*

---

# Tie It All Together: A Summary Chart for Cutting

**Name of block design:** *Evening Star*

| Which fabrics? | Fabric swatch[a] | How many squares? | How big? | Patch form involved? |
|---|---|---|---|---|
| **A** | | 4 | 3⅞″ × 3⅞″ | *2-Triangle* |
| | | | | |
| | | | | |
| **B** | | 4 | 3½″ × 3½″ | *1-Patch* |
| | | | | |
| | | | | |
| **C** (Beige) | | 4 | 3⅞″ × 3⅞″ | *2-Triangle* |
| | | 4 | 3½″ × 3½″ | *1-Patch* |
| | | | | |

[a] Color or paste in the fabric swatches to match your swatched paste-up.

## Crosses and Losses

- 16 Squares
- 24 Patches
- 2 Patch forms
- 8 Pieced squares
- 8 Whole-cloth squares
- 8 Bias seams
- 6 Converging seams
- 12 Thicknesses of fabric

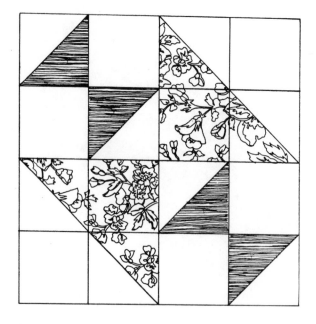

*52. Swatched paste-up for Crosses and Losses (see also color page E). Use your own fabrics and substitute them in a blank 16-square Choose a Design chart, copied from the one in the Appendix, to make your own swatched paste-up.*

# Tie It All Together: A Summary Chart for Cutting

**Name of block design:** *Crosses and Losses*

| Which fabrics? | Fabric swatch[a] | How many squares? | How big? | Patch form involved? |
|---|---|---|---|---|
| **A** | | *2* | *3½" × 3½"* | *1-Patch* |
| | | *2* | *3⅞" × 3⅞"* | *2-Triangle* |
| | | | | |
| **B** | | *2* | *3⅞" × 3⅞"* | *2-Triangle* |
| | | | | |
| | | | | |
| **C** (**Light pink**) | | *4* | *3⅞" × 3⅞"* | *2-Triangle* |
| | | *6* | *3½" × 3½"* | *1-Patch* |
| | | | | |

[a] Color or paste in the fabric swatches to match your swatched paste-up.

136

## Double 4-Patch

- 16 Squares
- 20 Patches
- 2 Patch forms
- 4 Pieced squares
- 12 Whole-cloth squares
- 4 Bias seams
- 5 Converging seams
- 10 Thicknesses of fabric

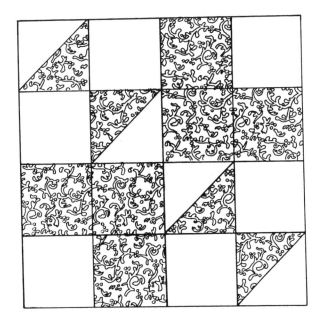

*53. Swatched paste-up for Double 4-Patch (see also color page G). Use your own fabrics and substitute them in a blank 16-square Choose a Design chart, copied from the one in the Appendix, to make your own swatched paste-up.*

---

## Tie It All Together: A Summary Chart for Cutting

**Name of block design:** *Double 4-Patch*

| Which fabrics? | Fabric swatch[a] | How many squares? | How big? | Patch form involved? |
|---|---|---|---|---|
| **A** | | 6 | $3\frac{1}{2}'' \times 3\frac{1}{2}''$ | 1-Patch |
| | | 2 | $3\frac{7}{8}'' \times 3\frac{7}{8}''$ | 2-Triangle |
| | | | | |
| **B** (Muslin) | | 2 | $3\frac{7}{8}'' \times 3\frac{7}{8}''$ | 2-Triangle |
| | | 6 | $3\frac{1}{2}'' \times 3\frac{1}{2}''$ | 1-Patch |
| | | | | |

[a] Color or paste in the fabric swatches to match your swatched paste-up.

## Helen's Choice

- 9 Squares
- 15 Patches
- 2 Patch forms
- 6 Pieced squares
- 3 Whole-cloth squares
- 6 Bias seams
- 6 Converging seams
- 12 Thicknesses of fabric

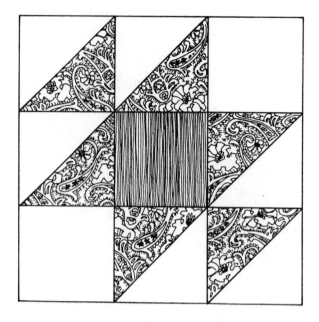

54. *Swatched paste-up for Helen's Choice (see also color page E). Use your own fabrics and substitute them in a blank 9-square Choose a Design chart, copied from the one in the Appendix, to make your own swatched paste-up.*

# Tie It All Together: A Summary Chart for Cutting

**Name of block design:** *Helen's Choice*

| Which fabrics? | Fabric swatch[a] | How many squares? | How big? | Patch form involved? |
|---|---|---|---|---|
| A | | 3 | 4⅞" × 4⅞" | 2-Triangle |
| | | | | |
| | | | | |
| B | | 1 | 4½" × 4½" | 1-Patch |
| | | | | |
| | | | | |
| C (Off white) | | 3 | 4⅞" × 4⅞" | 2-Triangle |
| | | 2 | 4½" × 4½" | 1-Patch |
| | | | | |

[a] Color or paste in the fabric swatches to match your swatched paste-up.

## Jacob's Ladder

- 9 Squares
- 28 Patches
- 2 Patch forms
- 9 Pieced squares
- 4 Bias seams
- 6 Converging seams
- 12 Thicknesses of fabric

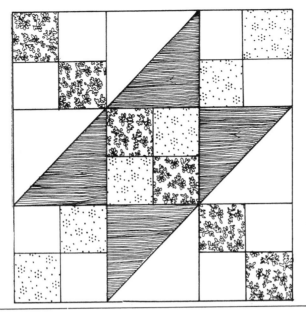

*55. Swatched paste-up for Jacob's Ladder (see also color page B). Use your own fabrics and substitute them in a blank 9-square Choose a Design chart, copied from the one in the Appendix, to make your own swatched paste-up.*

# Tie It All Together: A Summary Chart for Cutting

**Name of block design:** *Jacob's Ladder*

| Which fabrics? | Fabric swatch[a] | How many? | How big? | Patch form involved? |
|---|---|---|---|---|
| **A** (Rust) | | 2 Squares | 4⅞" × 4⅞" | 2-Triangle |
| **B** | | 3 Rectangles | 2½" × 5" | 4-Square |
| **C** | | 3 Rectangles | 2½" × 5" | 4-Square |
| **D** (Off white) | | 2 Squares | 4⅞" × 4⅞" | 2-Triangle |
| | | 4 Rectangles | 2½" × 5" | 4-Square |

[a] Color or paste in the fabric swatches to match your swatched paste-up.

139

# King's Crown

- 16 Squares
- 24 Patches
- 2 Patch forms
- 8 Pieced squares
- 8 Whole-cloth squares
- 8 Bias seams
- 6 Converging seams
- 12 Thicknesses of fabric

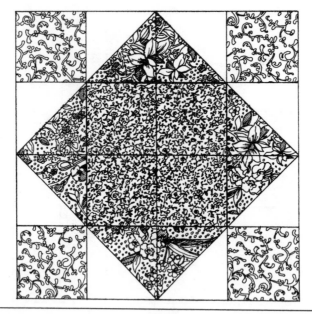

56. *Swatched paste-up for King's Crown (see also color page A). Use your own fabrics and substitute them in a blank 16-square Choose a Design chart, copied from the one in the Appendix, to make your own swatched paste-up.*

## Tie It All Together: A Summary Chart for Cutting

Name of block design: _King's Crown_

| Which fabrics? | Fabric swatch[a] | How many squares? | How big? | Patch form involved? |
|---|---|---|---|---|
| A | | 4 | $3^7/8'' \times 3^7/8''$ | 2-Triangle |
| | | | | |
| | | | | |
| B | | 4 | $3^1/2'' \times 3^1/2''$ | 1-Patch |
| | | | | |
| | | | | |
| C | | 4 | $3^1/2'' \times 3^1/2''$ | 1-Patch |
| | | | | |
| | | | | |
| D (Beige) | | 4 | $3^7/8'' \times 3^7/8''$ | 2-Triangle |
| | | | | |
| | | | | |

[a] Color or paste in the fabric swatches to match your swatched paste-up.

140

## Old Maid's Puzzle

- 16 Squares
- 26 Patches
- 2 Patch forms
- 10 Pieced squares
- 6 Whole-cloth squares
- 10 Bias seams
- 6 Converging seams
- 12 Thicknesses of fabric

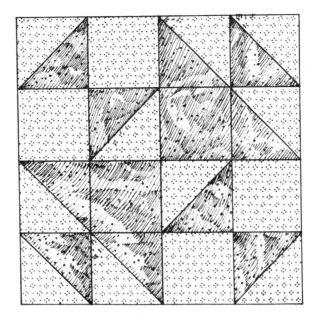

*57. Swatched paste-up for Old Maid's Puzzle (see also color page A). Use your own fabrics and substitute them in a blank 16-square Choose a Design chart, copied from the one in the Appendix, to make your own swatched paste-up.*

---

# Tie It All Together: A Summary Chart for Cutting

**Name of block design:** *Old Maid's Puzzle*

| Which fabrics? | Fabric swatch[a] | How many squares? | How big? | Patch form involved? |
|---|---|---|---|---|
| **A** (Blue) | | 2 | 3½″ × 3½″ | 1-Patch |
| | | 5 | 3⅞″ × 3⅞″ | 2-Triangle |
| | | | | |
| **B** | | 4 | 3½″ × 3½″ | 1-Patch |
| | | 5 | 3⅞″ × 3⅞″ | 2-Triangle |
| | | | | |

[a] Color or paste in the fabric swatches to match your swatched paste-up.

141

## Puss in the Corner

- 16 Squares
- 20 Patches
- 2 Patch forms
- 4 Pieced squares
- 12 Whole-cloth squares
- 4 Bias seams
- 4 Converging seams
- 8 Thicknesses of fabric

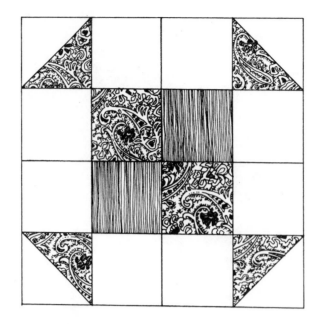

*58. Swatched paste-up for Puss in the Corner (see also color page H). Use your own fabrics and substitute them in a blank 16-square Choose a Design chart, copied from the one in the Appendix, to make your own swatched paste-up.*

---

# Tie It All Together: A Summary Chart for Cutting

**Name of block design:** *Puss in the Corner*

| Which fabrics? | Fabric swatch[a] | How many squares? | How big? | Patch form involved? |
|---|---|---|---|---|
| **A** | | 2 | $3\frac{1}{2}'' \times 3\frac{1}{2}''$ | 1-Patch |
| | | 2 | $3\frac{7}{8}'' \times 3\frac{7}{8}''$ | 2-Triangle |
| | | | | |
| **B** (Wine red) | | 2 | $3\frac{1}{2}'' \times 3\frac{1}{2}''$ | 1-Patch |
| | | | | |
| | | | | |
| **C** (Off white) | | 8 | $3\frac{1}{2}'' \times 3\frac{1}{2}''$ | 1-Patch |
| | | 2 | $3\frac{7}{8}'' \times 3\frac{7}{8}''$ | 2-Triangle |
| | | | | |

[a] Color or paste in the fabric swatches to match your swatched paste-up.

142

## Road to Oklahoma

- 16 Squares
- 20 Patches
- 2 Patch forms
- 4 Pieced squares
- 12 Whole-cloth squares
- 4 Bias seams
- 5 Converging seams
- 10 Thicknesses of fabric

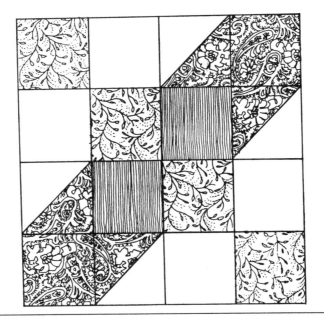

59. Swatched paste-up for Road to Oklahoma (see also color page C). Use your own fabrics and substitute them in a blank 16-square Choose a Design chart, copied from the one in the Appendix, to make your own swatched paste-up.

# Tie It All Together: A Summary Chart for Cutting

Name of block design: _Road to Oklahoma_

| Which fabrics? | Fabric swatch[a] | How many squares? | How big? | Patch form involved? |
|---|---|---|---|---|
| A | | 2 | $3\frac{1}{2}'' \times 3\frac{1}{2}''$ | 1-Patch |
| | | 2 | $3\frac{7}{8}'' \times 3\frac{7}{8}''$ | 2-Triangle |
| | | | | |
| B (Rust print) | | 4 | $3\frac{1}{2}'' \times 3\frac{1}{2}''$ | 1-Patch |
| | | | | |
| | | | | |
| C (Gray) | | 2 | $3\frac{1}{2}'' \times 3\frac{1}{2}''$ | 1-Patch |
| | | | | |
| | | | | |
| D (Beige) | | 4 | $3\frac{1}{2}'' \times 3\frac{1}{2}''$ | 1-Patch |
| | | 2 | $3\frac{7}{8}'' \times 3\frac{7}{8}''$ | 2-Triangle |
| | | | | |

[a] Color or paste in the fabric swatches to match your swatched paste-up.

# Ship

- 16 Squares
- 22 Patches
- 2 Patch forms
- 6 Pieced squares
- 10 Whole-cloth squares
- 6 Bias seams
- 5 Converging seams
- 10 Thicknesses of fabric

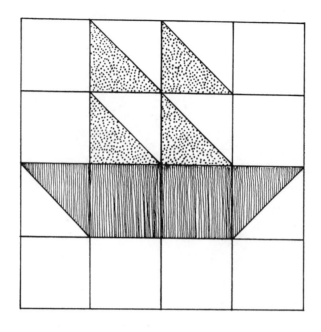

*60. Swatched paste-up for Ship (see also color page D). Use your own fabrics and substitute them in a blank 16-square Choose a Design chart, copied from the one in the Appendix, to make your own swatched paste-up.*

## Tie It All Together: A Summary Chart for Cutting

**Name of block design:** *Ship*

| Which fabrics? | Fabric swatch[a] | How many squares? | How big? | Patch form involved? |
|---|---|---|---|---|
| **A** (Blue) | | *2* | *3½″ × 3½″* | *1-Patch* |
| | | *1* | *3⅞″ × 3⅞″* | *2-Triangle* |
| | | | | |
| **B** (Red print) | | *2* | *3⅞″ × 3⅞″* | *2-Triangle* |
| | | | | |
| | | | | |
| **C** (Muslin) | | *8* | *3½″ × 3½″* | *1-Patch* |
| | | *3* | *3⅞″ × 3⅞″* | *2-Triangle* |
| | | | | |

[a] Color or paste in the fabric swatches to match your swatched paste-up.

144

## Shoofly

- 9 Squares
- 13 Patches
- 2 Patch forms
- 4 Pieced squares
- 5 Whole-cloth squares
- 4 Bias seams
- 4 Converging seams
- 8 Thicknesses of fabric

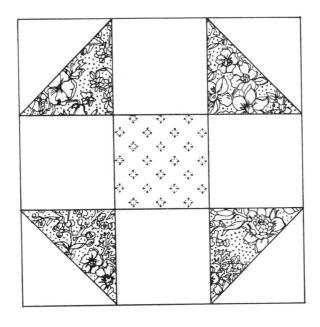

61. *Swatched paste-up for Shoofly (see also color page C). Use your own fabrics and substitute them in a blank 9-square Choose a Design chart, copied from the one in the Appendix, to make your own swatched paste-up.*

## Tie It All Together: A Summary Chart for Cutting

Name of block design: *Shoofly*

| Which fabrics? | Fabric swatch[a] | How many squares? | How big? | Patch form involved? |
|---|---|---|---|---|
| A | | *2* | *4⅞″ × 4⅞″* | *2-Triangle* |
| | | | | |
| | | | | |
| B (Orange print) | | *1* | *4½″ × 4½″* | *1-Patch* |
| | | | | |
| | | | | |
| C (Off white) | | *2* | *4⅞″ × 4⅞″* | *2-Triangle* |
| | | *4* | *4½″ × 4½″* | *1-Patch* |
| | | | | |

[a] Color or paste in the fabric swatches to match your swatched paste-up.

145

## Triplet

- 9 Squares
- 18 Patches
- 2 Patch forms
- 3 Pieced squares
- 6 Whole-cloth squares
- 6 Bias seams
- 6 Converging seams
- 12 Thicknesses of fabric

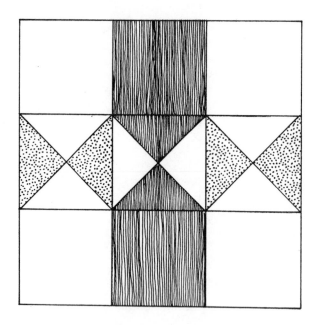

62. *Swatched paste-up for Triplet (see also color page D). Use your own fabrics and substitute them in a blank 9-square Choose a Design chart, copied from the one in the Appendix, to make your own swatched paste-up.*

## Tie It All Together: A Summary Chart for Cutting

**Name of block design:** _Triplet_

| Which fabrics? | Fabric swatch[a] | How many squares? | How big? | Patch form involved? |
|---|---|---|---|---|
| **A** (Blue) | | _2_ | _4½" × 4½"_ | _1-Patch_ |
| | | _1_ | _5⅜" × 5⅜"_ | _4-Triangle_ |
| | | | | |
| **B** (Red print) | | _2_ | _5⅜" × 5⅜"_ | _4-Triangle_ |
| | | | | |
| | | | | |
| **C** (Muslin) | | _4_ | _4½" × 4½"_ | _1-Patch_ |
| | | _3_ | _5⅜" × 5⅜"_ | _4-Triangle_ |
| | | | | |

[a] Color or paste in the fabric swatches to match your swatched paste-up.

## Windmill

- 16 Squares
- 20 Patches
- 2 Patch forms
- 4 Pieced squares
- 12 Whole-cloth squares
- 4 Bias seams
- 8 Converging seams
- 16 Thicknesses of fabric

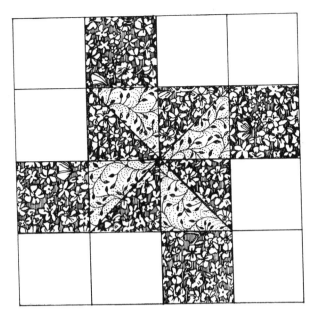

*63. Swatched paste-up for Windmill (see also color page A). Use your own fabrics and substitute them in a blank 16-square Choose a Design chart, copied from the one in the Appendix, to make your own swatched paste-up.*

---

## Tie It All Together: A Summary Chart for Cutting

**Name of block design:** *Windmill*

| Which fabrics? | Fabric swatch[a] | How many squares? | How big? | Patch form involved? |
|---|---|---|---|---|
| **A** (Blue print) | | 4 | 3½″ × 3½″ | Whole-cloth |
| | | 2 | 3⅞″ × 3⅞″ | 2-Triangle |
| | | | | |
| **B** (Red print) | | 2 | 3⅞″ × 3⅞″ | 2-Triangle |
| | | | | |
| | | | | |
| **C** (Beige) | | 8 | 3½″ × 3½″ | Whole-cloth |
| | | | | |
| | | | | |

[a] Color or paste in the fabric swatches to match your swatched paste-up.

## Closing Statement

Even though we do come to the end of a text as such, it is not, I hope, the end of your piecing of patchwork. As a matter of fact, you now have all of the learning experiences necessary to launch out on your own doing of the 24 sew-easy designs contained in the book. Once you have completed a number of blocks sufficient to form a quilt for a bed, wall hanging, or sofa quilt, you will be ready for the second aspect of quilting—the *setting of blocks* for a quilt. The actual sewing of quilt lines, quilting per se, is the last stage of what usually is referred to as "quilting." I hope that you will find both aspects of the total to be sew easy.

# Appendix of Blank Forms

## Choose a Design: 9 Squares

This illustration serves as a kind of road map. It shows you *where* you are going. It tells you *when* you get there. Duplicate the design you wish to construct within the reduced block form. Color or paste in swatches of the fabrics you have selected.

**Name of block design:** _____

# Choose a Design: 16 Squares

This illustration serves as a kind of road map. It shows you *where* you are going. It tells you *when* you get there. Duplicate the design you wish to construct within the reduced block form. Color or paste in swatches of the fabrics you have selected.

**Name of block design:** _____

# Look and See (Form and Color): 9 Squares

### Name of block design:

_____

When you can visualize a total block design in squares and patches, the entire process of patchworking—planning, cutting, piecing, assembly—becomes sew easy it's fun to do. But planning comes first and in the order listed below:

- Draw in the design you wish to construct.
- Color or paste in swatches of your chosen fabrics.
- Number the squares 1 to 9 from left to right and top to bottom.
- Letter the fabrics A, B, C, D, etc.

# Look and See (Form and Color): 16 Squares

**Name of block design:** _____

When you can visualize a total block design in squares and patches, the entire process of patch-working—planning, cutting, piecing, assembly—becomes sew easy it's fun to do. But planning comes first, in the order listed below:

- Draw in the design you wish to construct.
- Color or paste in swatches of your chosen fabrics.
- Number the squares 1 to 16 from left to right and top to bottom.
- Letter the fabrics A, B, C, D, etc.

# List All the Givens (Basic Information)

**Name of block design:** _____

Study the design presented in "Choose a Design" and complete the following blanks:

Finished size of block design[a] _____

Total number of squares in block[b] _____

Finished size of each square _____

Total number of patches in block[c] _____

Number of different fabrics needed _____

See the square forms illustrated below. Write in the total number needed of each in the space provided.

Total number of square forms[b] _____

| **1-patch** | **2-triangle** | **4-triangle** | **3-triangle** | **4-square** |
|:---:|:---:|:---:|:---:|:---:|
| No. _____ | No. _____ | No. _____ | No. _____ | No. _____ |

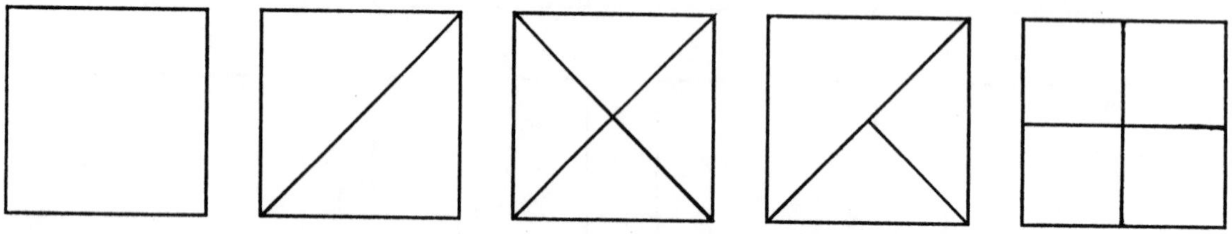

_____

[a] Finished size of all blocks in our book is 12″ × 12″.
[b] Total number of squares and total number of square forms must be the same.
[c] See the block designs in Figure 3 for this information (Chapter 3).

# Color Blocks Beautiful

Name of block design: _____

| Swatched square form[a] | How many in block design? | Placement in block design (square numbers) |
|---|---|---|
| ☐ | _____ | _____ |
| ☐ | _____ | _____ |
| ☐ | _____ | _____ |
| ☐ | _____ | _____ |

[a] Duplicate each square in the block design that *differs* from the others in form and/or color. (Use additional pages as necessary.)

# Square Things Away

**Name of block design:** _____

Look carefully at the block design illustrated in Look and See. The chart below indicates what you are to look for. Write down what you see in the spaces that are provided. Read each column heading carefully and double-check your counting.

| Square form | Number of whole-cloth squares in block design, by fabric | Number of squares to cut, by fabric | Cutting size of squares, by fabric[a] |
|---|---|---|---|
| **Whole-cloth** | **Fabric A** _____ | _____ | _____ |
| | **Fabric B** _____ | _____ | _____ |
| | **Fabric C** _____ | _____ | _____ |
| | **Fabric D** _____ | _____ | _____ |
| **Number in block design** _____ | **Fabric E** _____ | _____ | _____ |

[a] Cutting size = finished size + ½″ for whole-cloth squares.

| Square form | Number of triangles from 2-triangle squares, by fabric | Number of squares to cut, by fabric[b] | Cutting size of squares, by fabric[c] |
|---|---|---|---|
| **2-triangle** | **Fabric A** _____ | _____ | _____ |
| | **Fabric B** _____ | _____ | _____ |
| | **Fabric C** _____ | _____ | _____ |
| | **Fabric D** _____ | _____ | _____ |
| **Number in block design** _____ | **Fabric E** _____ | _____ | _____ |

[b] Number of triangles divided by 2 = number of squares to cut. A full square is required for any number of triangles less than 2.
[c] Cutting size = finished size of pieced square + ⅞″ for 2-triangle squares.

## Square Things Away, continued

| Square form | Number of triangles from 4-triangle squares, by fabric | Number of squares to cut, by fabric[d] | Cutting size of squares, by fabric[e] |
|---|---|---|---|
| **4-triangle** | Fabric A _____ | _____ | _____ |
| | Fabric B _____ | _____ | _____ |
| | Fabric C _____ | _____ | _____ |
| | Fabric D _____ | _____ | _____ |
| **Number in block design** _____ | Fabric E _____ | _____ | _____ |

[d] Number of triangles divided by 4 = number of squares to cut. A full square is required for any number of triangles less than 4.
[e] Cutting size = finished size of pieced square + 1⅜″.

| Square form | Number of triangles in 1-triangle half of squares, by fabric | Number of squares to cut, by fabric[f] | Cutting size of squares, by fabric[g] |
|---|---|---|---|
| **3-triangle** | Fabric A _____ | _____ | _____ |
| | Fabric B _____ | _____ | _____ |
| | Fabric C _____ | _____ | _____ |
| | Fabric D _____ | _____ | _____ |
| **Number in block design** _____ | Fabric E _____ | _____ | _____ |

[f] Number of triangles divided by 2 = the number of squares to cut for the 1-triangle half. A full square is required for any number of triangles less than 2.
[g] Cutting size = finished size + ⅞″.

## Square Things Away, continued

| Square form | Number of triangles in 2-triangle half of squares, by fabric | Number of squares to cut, by fabric[h] | Cutting size of squares, by fabric[i] |
|---|---|---|---|
| 3-triangle | Fabric A _____ | _____ | _____ |
| | Fabric B _____ | _____ | _____ |
| | Fabric C _____ | _____ | _____ |
| | Fabric D _____ | _____ | _____ |
| Number in block design _____ | Fabric E _____ | _____ | _____ |

[h] Number of triangles divided by 4 = number of squares to cut for the two-triangle half. A full square is required for any number of triangles less than 4.
[i] Cutting size = finished size + $1\frac{3}{8}''$.

| Square form | Number of small squares within the larger square, by fabric | Number of rectangles to cut, by fabric | Cutting size of squares, by fabric[j] |
|---|---|---|---|
| 4-square | Fabric A _____ | _____ | _____ |
| | Fabric B _____ | _____ | _____ |
| | Fabric C _____ | _____ | _____ |
| | Fabric D _____ | _____ | _____ |
| Number in block design _____ | Fabric E _____ | _____ | _____ |

[j] Cut two small squares together as a rectangle. See text page 97 for details.

# Tie It All Together: A Summary Chart for Cutting

Name of block design: _____

| Which fabrics? | Fabric swatch[a] | How many squares? | How big? | Patch form involved? |
|---|---|---|---|---|
| A | | _____ <br> _____ <br> _____ | _____ <br> _____ <br> _____ | _____ <br> _____ <br> _____ |
| B | | _____ <br> _____ <br> _____ | _____ <br> _____ <br> _____ | _____ <br> _____ <br> _____ |
| C | | _____ <br> _____ <br> _____ | _____ <br> _____ <br> _____ | _____ <br> _____ <br> _____ |
| D | | _____ <br> _____ <br> _____ | _____ <br> _____ <br> _____ | _____ <br> _____ <br> _____ |
| E | | _____ <br> _____ <br> _____ | _____ <br> _____ <br> _____ | _____ <br> _____ <br> _____ |

[a] Color or paste in the fabric swatches identified in Look and See.

## Personal Harmony Chart

| Name of Color Harmony | Beginning Color | Additional Colors for Blending |
|---|---|---|
| **MONOCHROMATIC**<br>Tint, shades, tones of one color—any color. Pattern added to avoid monotony. | | |
| **ANALOGOUS OR RELATED**<br>Made of two or more colors adjacent to each other on the color wheel. | | |
| **TRIADIC**<br>Made of any three colors that are equidistant on the color wheel. | | |
| **DIRECT COMPLEMENT**<br>Two colors that are directly opposite each other on the color wheel are direct complements. | | |
| **SPLIT COMPLEMENT**<br>One color plus two colors next to its complement create a split complement. | | |
| **DOUBLE COMPLEMENT**<br>Two adjacent colors plus both their complements together create a double complement. | | |

## Per-Yard Yield for Sew-Easy Designs with 9 Squares
### (45″ Wide Fabric)

| Square form | Cutting size of each square | Number squares in crosswise strip | Number strips per yard length | Yield per yard |
|---|---|---|---|---|
| Whole-cloth square | 4½″ × 4½″ | 10 | 8 | 80 |
| 2-triangle square | 4⅞″ × 4⅞″ | 9 | 7 | 63 |
| 4-triangle square | 5⅜″ × 5⅜″ | 7 | 6 | 42 |
| 3-triangle square | | | | |
| | 4⅞″ × 4⅞″ | 9 | 7 | 63 |
| | 5⅜″ × 5⅜″ | 7 | 6 | 42 |
| 4-square square | 2½″ × 5″ | 18 | 14 | 252 |

## Per-Yard Yield for Sew-Easy Designs with 16 Squares (45″ Wide Fabric)

| Square form | Cutting size of each square | Number squares in crosswise strip | Number strips per yard length | Yield per yard |
|---|---|---|---|---|
| Whole-cloth square | 3½″ × 3½″ | 12 | 10 | 120 |
| 2-triangle square | 3⅞″ × 3⅞″ | 11 | 9 | 99 |
| 4-triangle square | 4⅜″ × 4⅜″ | 10 | 8 | 80 |
| 3-triangle square ◿ | 3⅞″ × 3⅞″ | 11 | 9 | 99 |
| ◺ | 4⅜″ × 4⅜″ | 10 | 8 | 80 |
| 4-square square | 2″ × 4″ | 22 | 18 | 396 |

## Index